the power of kabbalah

Kabbalah Publishing is a registered DBA of
Kabbalah Centre International, Inc.

For further information:

The Kabbalah Centre
155 E. 48th St., New York, NY 10017
1062 S. Robertson Blvd., Los Angeles, CA 90035

1.800.Kabbalah www.kabbalah.com

First Edition
September 2000

Revised Edition
First Trade Paper
December 2010

Printed in Canada

ISBN13: 978-1-57189-699-5

Design: HL Design (Hyun Min Lee) www.hldesignco.com

Mixed Sources
Product group from well-managed forests,
controlled sources and recycled wood or fiber
www.fsc.org Cert no. SW-COC-000952
© 1996 Forest Stewardship Council
FSC

the
power
of
kabbalah

13 Principles to Overcome Challenges and Achieve Fulfillment

KABBALAH
PUBLISHING

yehuda berg

acknowledgement

First and foremost I would like to thank all the readers who made this book an international best seller. You have helped me to share this life-enhancing teaching with the world It is said that without a desire on the part of the student, the teacher cannot emerge.

Power of Kabbalah was my first book and it is the culmination of a lifetime of my father and mother's work and guidance. It is the product of my brother's support and wisdom, my wife's love, my children's faith in me, the friendship of my peers and the dedication of those who work for Kabbalah Publishing. To list the names of the people who made this book possible would run longer than the book itself. You know who you are. Thank you.

The 13 Principles of Kabbalah

One: Don't Believe a Word You Read. Test-Drive the Lessons Learned.

Two: Two Basic Realities Exist: Our 1 Percent World of Darkness and the 99 Percent Realm of Light.

Three: Everything That a Human Being Truly Desires from Life is Spiritual Light.

Four: The Purpose of Life is Spiritual Transformation from a Reactive Being to a Proactive Being.

Five: In the Moment of Our Transformation, We Make Contact With the 99 Percent Realm.

Six: Never—and That Means Never—Lay Blame on Other People or External Events.

Seven: Resisting Our Reactive Impulses Creates Lasting Light.

Eight: Reactive Behavior Creates Intense Sparks of Light, but Eventually Leaves Darkness in Its Wake.

Nine: Obstacles Are Our Opportunity to Connect to The Light.

Ten: The Greater the Obstacle, the Greater the Potential Light.

Eleven: When Challenges Appear Overwhelming, Inject Certainty. The Light is Always There.

Twelve: All of the Negative Traits That You Spot in Others Are Merely a Reflection of Your Own Negative Traits. Only By Changing Yourself Can You See a Change in Others.

Thirteen: "Love Thy Neighbor As Thyself. All the Rest is Mere Commentary. Now Go and Learn."

table of contents

introduction 1

part one: 15
who are we?

part two: 53
creation, the big bang, and the nature of god

part three: 81
the puzzle of creation and the theory of reactivity

part four: 121
the game, the opponent, and
the role of space and time

part five: 167
resistance and the art of transformation

part six: 197
correction, slavery and
the miraculous power of certainty

part seven: 221
winning the game of life

Exercises:
Applying the Transformation Formula 113
Removing Spiritual Blockages 134
Releasing Negative Feelings from the Past 163
Uncovering Your *Tikkun* 204

introduction

introduction

A man wakes up in the morning and decides to go fishing. He goes to the dock, sits down, pulls out his fishing line, and throws it in. On the dock, there's another fisherman who seems to be catching quite a few fish. With every fish this fisherman catches, he takes it to the side of the dock where there is a ruler. After measuring each fish, he keeps some and throws back others. After observing this behavior for some time, the first man approaches the other fisherman and says, "What's up? Why are you throwing some fish back and keeping others? What are you looking for?"

The other fisherman replies, "I've got a twelve-inch pot in my house. The only fish I keep are the ones under twelve inches. Fish that are bigger, I can't use, so I throw them away."

Like this fisherman, we limit ourselves without even realizing it. We're trying to fit the universe's infinite abundance into our small pot. The universe wants to give us everything, but we can't receive all that is available to us. What would happen if we expanded our vessel instead of placing limits on our abundance?

We can get more in our lives if we become more. I'm amazed sometimes by how small, how limited, our thinking can be. When someone asks us what we want out of the whole universe, we find ourselves saying that we want some little thing, just this or that.

It's time to upgrade our vessel in order to receive more by acknowledging what will truly give us fulfillment.

What do you really want from life?

I've asked this question of many people around the world, and it's remarkable how universal the answers are. People want more money, a nice car, a comfortable house, and good health. They will say they want more fulfillment, happiness, and passion, but they're not always interested in doing the deeper work required to bring those things into their lives.

We often attempt to bring a sense of excitement into our life through some kind of external stimulus. A cigarette. Drugs. Alcohol. Food. All these substances give us a sense of temporary satisfaction. Then along comes Kabbalah with its simple, powerful message: You're never going to know true meaning and purpose if you keep trying to add up smaller and smaller experiences of short-lived excitement. That's not how it works. Kabbalah encourages us to expand who we are in order to achieve a lasting flow of fulfillment—not the fleeting variety that lets us down again and again.

We live in trying times. We watch the news and hear how someone just killed his entire family or how a child was raised for decades in a locked basement. Global warming is generating record-breaking storms and extreme weather. Our water is in low supply or contaminated. The world has gone crazy. At the same time, there is more spiritual Light and information being revealed than ever before. These two realities are occurring simultaneously: revelation and darkness. And this is one of the reasons why spiritual concepts are gaining importance in public awareness these days. Fifty years ago, no one even knew the word Kabbalah, let alone what it meant. Today, there are millions of people studying it. We need this wisdom now more than ever because of the chaos that is thriving in the world today.

We turn to Kabbalah because the antidote for chaos can be found there.

the power of kabbalah

There are many myths and misconceptions about Kabbalah. One of the most widespread is that one must be Jewish, male, and a rabbinical scholar over the age of 40 to study it. In the past, that was true in part, because the information Kabbalah offered was so complex. People were also being killed simply for having this wisdom. Why? Because any new technology can be seen as very threatening.

Imagine traveling back in time to, say, the 15th century, and showing people your Blackberry or iPhone. They would think you were a witch or a wizard. The teaching of Kabbalah has made people feel the same way. I was thrown out of school a few times because my father was a kabbalist. My parents have been physically attacked. My mom was beaten to the point of suffering a concussion because of her decision to share Kabbalah with everyone who wanted to learn from it.

But you know what? Nothing, and no one, has been able to stop this knowledge from coming out.

Although religion was given to humankind to unify us, to bring us together for a higher purpose, it hasn't worked out that way. Nothing has caused more separation and destruction than organized religion. Its self-righteousness and divisiveness have led to countless wars and mass bloodshed. Wisdom, on the other hand, encourages us to come together as one, to use our connection to the Creator—God, Allah, Jesus, Buddha, or whatever you want to call the God-force—to unite under its energy.

So why is this wisdom different from religion? For one thing, it is totally opposed to blind faith. Kabbalists believe that we have to question everything and then make sure what we've learned is working for us.

We have to try everything, do the work, be open. At the end of these chapters, see if you haven't made a significant change in your understanding of life, in your appreciation of everything you already have, in the excitement and newness of removing old layers of negativity. If what you have learned isn't working for you, then close this book and put it on the shelf. You decide whether studying Kabbalah is worth it or not.

There is a wonderful story about a student of Zen Buddhism who circled the globe looking for a teacher. Finally, he discovered a famous Zen master and went to see him. The student was so excited about meeting with the master that he tried to tell him everything he knew. As the student was rambling on, the Zen master asked, "Do you want some tea?" The student replied, "Yes." The master started pouring the tea. The student kept on talking. He saw that the cup was full, but the Zen master was continuing to pour, spilling tea all over the table. Perplexed, the student said, "Master, the cup is full. Why do you keep on pouring?" The master replied, "The cup is a lot like you. You are so full of wisdom already that there is no room for anything else to go in."

a fountainhead of wisdom: the lineage of kabbalah

The first kabbalist was Abraham, who wrote *The Book of Formation*. Abraham is known in the Bible as the father of religion, but he was also a kabbalist. Next came Moses, who not only brought down the physical Ten Commandments and spiritual knowledge in the form of the Bible, but also taught practical kabbalistic tools for living a good life.

The oral tradition of Moses was passed from teacher to student, again and again, until some 2000 years ago when Rav Shimon bar Yochai authored the foundational sacred text of Kabbalah, the *Zohar*. The *Zohar* is an acknowledged source of great spiritual wisdom that is as ancient as the Bible itself; indeed, the *Zohar* is known as the "decoder of the Bible." But the world wasn't ready for the language and technology it offered, so the *Zohar* then remained hidden for over 1200 years. The study of the *Zohar* is called Kabbalah.

Around the 14th century, Kabbalah started to emerge from complete secrecy. The actual *Zohar* is said to have been dug up by the Knights Templar in Jerusalem and brought back to Europe. This is when the power of the *Zohar* began making itself known. Interestingly, it was at this time that the Grail legend first appeared. Some say that the Holy Grail is a book, possibly the *Zohar*, but this is only speculation, however intriguing.

Since then, some very famous people have studied the *Zohar*. Sir Isaac Newton, for example, had his own version of the *Zohar* in Latin, and he noted that Plato went to Egypt to study the *Zohar* there. Another great thinker who studied the *Zohar* was Pythagoras, who would climb Mount Carmel dressed in white like a high priest and meditate.

Why were these prominent thinkers so taken with the *Zohar*? Because it explains the spiritual and physical laws of the universe and our lives. The *Zohar* reveals the secrets of our world and answers the age-old questions: What is the purpose of life? Why was the world created? How was the world created? Why am I here? Indeed, the *Zohar's* principles can be found in the words and writings of Jesus, Muhammad, Moses, and Buddha.

As we've seen, kabbalists have been persecuted for their efforts to make the *Zohar* available to all people. After their passing, however, these same kabbalists were discovered to be righteous individuals by the very people who had maligned them. This has been the story of the revelation of Kabbalah for centuries. In 1922, Rav Ashlag founded The Kabbalah Centre. His efforts, too, were met with violent opposition. Upon his passing, he handed the leadership of The Centre to his student, Rav Brandwein, who would later pass the mantle on to his beloved student, Rav Berg. Rav Berg is my father. Thanks to his selfless effort and that of my mother, Karen, I have the freedom to write this book, and you can now gain access to the power of studying Kabbalah.

One special quality found in the lineage of The Kabbalah Centre is that these great scholars have made the *Zohar* and its teachings available in a language that the layperson can readily understand. Their intent was not to win a Nobel Prize, but rather to bring simple happiness, permanent peace, and never-ending fulfillment to all humanity. It may seem to us today that the *Zohar* has always been accessible and readily available to everyone everywhere. But just a few short decades ago, you could not have found these books nor studied their wisdom for any amount of money; indeed, even the attempt to do so might have led to your being vilified, beaten, or worse.

please be warned

There remains in effect a single warning, a strict prohibition concerning the study of Kabbalah. This warning dates from the second century, and it is the first of the Thirteen Principles of Kabbalah that will be presented in this book:

> Principle One:
> **Don't Believe a Word You Read. Test-Drive the Lessons Learned.**

Some say the *Zohar* is not just a light at the end of the tunnel, but the Light that removes the tunnel itself, opening up whole new dimensions of meaning and awareness. The *Zohar* tells us many things: how and why the world began; why it is so difficult to break negative patterns that cause us such pain; why we continue to avoid the activities that we know are good for us in our lives; why chaos bothers to exist; how to instill meaning and generate spiritual power into every waking moment. These are impressive promises, but don't believe one word of them. Not for one second.

Belief implies the potential for doubt, but true *knowing* leaves no opportunity for skepticism. Knowing means certainty, complete conviction—in your gut, in your heart, in your soul. In order to know something, you need to try it out for yourself. So test each lesson in this book. Apply its principles to your life. Live the wisdom, and see if your life gets better. Testing is an important part of Kabbalah, part of a key precept that states: "No coercion in spirituality."

The intent of this book is not to preach, but to humbly teach. For this reason, I ask you to not take these lessons on faith. Instead, look for tangible results in your personal experiences. When you find them, you will come to *know* the wisdom in your heart.

the language of simplicity

In writing *The Power of Kabbalah*, I meant it to be a book that is both lighthearted and profound, so that in reading it, you would experience both fun and insight at the same time. Wisdom does not have to be complex and heavy. My father taught me something important at a very young age: When striving to understand the mysteries of our universe and the truth of our existence, how will we know if something is indeed truthful? The litmus test is simplicity. Authentic truth is comprehensible to everyone, even children.

A wise person is one who knows how to make complicated matters simple.

misconceptions about kabbalah

Those who danced were thought to be quite insane
by those who could not hear the music.
— Angela Monet

It was once thought that the study of Kabbalah could drive people to madness. Kabbalah is the science of the soul, the physics (and metaphysics) of fulfillment. But because it was a practical, innovative wisdom that appeared on the scene thousands of years before its time, it was branded by misunderstanding.

What was once considered mysticism is now called science or technology. As the renowned writer Arthur C. Clarke put it: "Any sufficiently advanced technology is indistinguishable from magic."

part one
who are we?

the makeup of humanity

Who and what are we? Did you ever stop and truly contemplate this question? What is our basic makeup? What is our substance? What essential element are we made of? The answer, in a word:

Desire

we are desire in motion

When I use the word *desire* to define us, it is not a metaphor. Desire is the essential quality of our human nature. It is the stuff we're made of. It is what drives us and makes us tick. We are all bundles of desire, constantly seeking to fulfill ourselves. Our heart beats, our blood flows, our body moves, solely because of an urge seeking to be fulfilled. Think of how a newborn comes into this world. What is its first instinct? It wants. It cries. It calls out to receive. This is nature, and for good reason. A newborn must receive clothing, comfort, sustenance, food, and shelter to survive. If we don't receive all those things, we simply won't make it.

desire and diversity

Once we get beyond infancy, it is our unique desires that give us our individual identity. Some people desire sexual fulfillment. Some seek spiritual enrichment. Some of us desire fame. Others seek solitude. Some want to achieve enlightenment, while others look for travel and adventure. Many think wealth will satiate their appetite. And there are those who pursue academia to quench their thirst for knowledge.

Three Levels of Human Desires

Level One

These desires are rooted in lust. The Level One person's needs, wants, and learned behaviors are focused on gratifying his or her primal animal urges. The desire to eat and sleep, and the craving for sex (not love) are all Level One desires. People at Level One may make use of rational, intellectual thought, as all human beings do, but they do so primarily to serve their most basic needs.

Level Two

These desires are directed toward the kinds of fulfillment not found in the animal kingdom, such goals as honor, power, prestige, fame, and dominion over others. Consequently, the thoughts, conscious choices, decisions, and actions of people at Level Two are directed toward gratifying to the fullest extent these desires for status.

Level Three

The desires at this level are driven mainly by the higher faculties of reasoning and are oriented toward gratifying to the fullest such intellectually driven desires as the yearning for wisdom, knowledge, and answers.

"These three types of desire," Rav Ashlag states, "are found in all members of the human race; however, they are blended in each individual to different degrees, and this is the difference between one person and another."

a vessel

In the language of Kabbalah, desire is referred to as a *Vessel*. A Vessel is like an empty cup that seeks to be filled. Unlike an empty cup, however, the Vessel of our desires is not anything physical. Remember the time when you were so full you couldn't eat another bite, but when the dessert cart was wheeled to your table, your desire for something sweet became overwhelming? The next thing you knew, you were gobbling up Black Forest cake. Your stomach has its limits, but there is no limit to your desire.

Every action in this physical world is directed by an urge, large or small, yearning to be fulfilled. It's as though we have no free will in the matter. We live life on autopilot, driven by the constant need to nourish all the longings that linger in both our body and our soul.

the object of our desire

So if our taste buds want dessert, what does our heart truly desire? It would be safe to say that the primary objective of our heart's desire is constant, uninterrupted happiness, although the definition of happiness may mean something different to each person.

Our desire for happiness unifies us all. You don't have to convince a criminal, a lawyer, a construction worker, a CEO, a wicked person, a kind person, an atheist, a pious person, a mogul, or a pauper to want happiness. The desire for endless happiness is part of our very essence as human beings.

A scientist might desire truth and an understanding of the laws that govern our physical world, or may be looking for a Nobel Prize and a permanent place in history. A politician may desire to improve his or her community, city, state, or country, or may opt instead for personal privilege, influence, and prominence. A child generally desires play and pleasure. A stand-up comic might desire laughter, love, fame, and acceptance. A businessperson usually desires financial success. A factory worker may want a vacation, food on the table, or peace of mind. Scholars generally desire knowledge and acclaim from their academic peers.

However different they may sound, all the objects of our desire are really just differently shaped packages of happiness. These various containers of contentment set us in motion and shape our lives.

All these different packages can also be described by one other word:

Light!

the power of light

Light is a code word, a metaphor to convey the broad spectrum of fulfillment that human beings long for. When a shaft of sunlight strikes a droplet of water in a sun shower, the light refracts into the colors of the rainbow. Think about this image. Just as this single ray of sunlight includes all the colors of the spectrum, Light contains all the "colors" of joy and fulfillment that people seek in their lives.

There is an important distinction, however, between sunlight and Light described by the Zohar. The light of the sun includes a mere seven primary colors in its spectrum, while Light contains every conceivable form of fulfillment and pleasure that a soul can yearn for. This includes the joy of sex and the ecstasy of chocolate, the vitality of good health and the power of prosperity, the joy of parenting and the bliss of a loving, passionate relationship.

Light is also the voice we call intuition, the magic that attracts the right people and right opportunities into our lives, the force that activates our immune system, the inner spirit that arouses perseverance and optimism within us each morning, and the fuel that generates our motivation to seek more and more out of life.

the light stays on

But Light is not just happiness. Light is *unending* happiness. It's the difference between momentary pleasure and lasting fulfillment. We don't really want a short-lived, pleasurable high. Our deepest desires are not limited to 15 minutes of fame, or a brief rush from closing a great business deal, or a temporary high from drugs, or the interim relief from a painkiller. We don't want to be liked by our friends and colleagues for just a moment. We don't want to be healthy for only half of our life. We don't want passionate sexual relations with our spouse for just the first few months of a 25-year-relationship. We want our desires to be constantly fulfilled, and it is this continuous, unending flow of fulfillment that the *Zohar* defines as Light.

the root of our unhappiness

The reason we are unhappy and anxious is because our desires are not constantly fulfilled by Light. If we have joy in one area of our life for five years, we may feel fortunate, but this also means there was enough Light in the "tank" to last for only five years. Running out of Light—or rather, disconnecting from Light—makes us unhappy. The more Light we have in our life, the longer our desires remain fulfilled and the happier we are.

We also have a lingering, deep-seated fear that our happiness will eventually end. When we find ourselves in a rare state of contentment and serenity, we have a negative tendency to believe it's too good to be true. We worry about tomorrow. And the moment these doubts creep in, we lose our connection to the Light. Light is therefore also defined as the peace of mind that comes from knowing that happiness will still be with us tomorrow. When we are connected to the Light, we have no fear, anxiety, or insecurity about the future.

ultimate desire

In light of the above (pun intended), we understand that a human being's ultimate desire is for Light. Moreover, this Light we seek is everywhere. It is the most common substance in our universe. It fills the cosmos and saturates our reality. The Light is infinite, boundless, and always ready to fulfill us. Which leads us to the obvious question:

If people are the essence of desire,
and what we desire is Light,
since the universe is flooded with Light,
then what stands in the way of our everlasting happiness?

A curtain.

two sides of the curtain: the 1 percent realm and the 99 percent realm

There is a curtain that divides our existence into two realms, which the wisdom of Kabbalah identifies as the 1 Percent Realm and the 99 Percent Realm.

The 1 Percent Realm encompasses the physical world, which is only a tiny part of all Creation. It is what we perceive with our five senses— what we smell, taste, touch, see, and hear. And although it may seem like a lot to us, what we experience with our five senses is a mere fragment of what is truly out there.

A Brief Summary of the 1 Percent

The 1 Percent Reality is the physical world we experience with our five senses. Spiritually, it is a realm of darkness, where:

- We react to external events;
- Fulfillment is temporary;
- Symptoms and reactions preoccupy us;
- We are victims who suffer because of other people's actions as well as random external circumstances;
- There appears to be no hope for bringing about permanent, positive change; and
- The majority of our desires remain unfulfilled.

Murphy's Law governs the realm of the 1 Percent: Everything that can possibly go wrong will go wrong. Even when things go well, we know they'll change because we live in the dimension of up and down, of good news and bad news.

When we live our lives solely in the 1 Percent, life hurts, and the world appears dark and disordered.

On the other side of the curtain lies the 99 Percent Dimension, which encompasses the vast majority of reality.

A Brief Summary of the 99 Percent

The 99 Percent Reality lies beyond human perception. It is:

- A world of absolute order, perfection, and infinite spiritual Light;
- A realm of action rather than reaction;
- The source, the seed, and the hidden origin of the physical world;
- A world of total fulfillment, infinite knowledge, and endless joy; and
- A dimension in which we can initiate positive, lasting change that also manifests in our 1 Percent World.

There is no trace of Murphy's Law in the realm of the 99 Percent. When we live connecting to the 99 Percent Level, life is fulfilling, energy flows, and the world is bright and beautiful.

So now we have arrived at the Second Principle of Kabbalah:

> ## Principle Two:
> ## Two Basic Realities Exist: Our 1 Percent World of Darkness and the 99 Percent Realm of Light.

20th Century Science Stumbles upon the 99 Percent

Stuart Hameroff, M.D., is a professor of anesthesiology and psychology, and the associate director of the Center for Consciousness Studies at the University of Arizona. Together with renowned Oxford physicist Sir Roger Penrose, Professor Hameroff observed that the understanding of the 99 Percent Realm is remarkably similar to our contemporary quantum mechanical view of the universe.

In an interview that I conducted with him for this book, Dr. Hameroff put it this way:

> For 100 years, it has been known that there exist two worlds: the classical world we experience with our five senses and the quantum world. We live in the classical world where everything seems "normal" (if unfulfilling). Everything has a definite shape, place, and substance. However, at very small scales, the quantum world reigns and everything is strange and bizarre, defying common sense.
>
> Science knows very little about the quantum world, but we now believe that the quantum world is a vast storage house of information including Platonic values such as good versus evil, beauty, truth, and wisdom. To me,

31

these are indications that the quantum world qualifies as the 99 percent reality that Kabbalah speaks of, and that a curtain does indeed exist between the two worlds.

Another way of putting this is that although the 99 Percent Realm is undetected and undetectable by the five senses, it is far more real than our physical world.

the suddenly syndrome

In the 1 Percent Realm, life constantly catches us off guard. We are afflicted with the Suddenly Syndrome. How many times have you heard the following?

- He died of a *sudden* heart attack.
- He walked out on her *without a word of warning*.
- The deal *suddenly* fell through.
- She *suddenly* changed her mind.
- Life *suddenly* felt so empty.

But is there really such a thing as "suddenly"? Not if you are aware of how things function in the 99 Percent World. There is always a concealed, unseen cause that precedes any "sudden" event.

Did you ever wake up one morning to suddenly find a full-grown oak tree standing tall on your front lawn? Of course not. Sometime in the past, an oak tree seed was planted. Likewise, when a nasty problem suddenly pops up and cuts off the flow of happiness that was fulfilling a particular desire, this is not just a random event. There exists a deeper cause. Sometime in the past, a seed was planted. I believe that there are no mistakes, no coincidences, no accidents, no sudden catastrophes. This is a cause-and-effect world.

Whatever happens, happens for a reason.

chaos theory

The Suddenly Syndrome stems from our inability to see through the illusions of the 1 Percent Realm. We cannot see beyond the immediate turmoil of our physical world to the other side of the curtain where the larger reality resides.

For years, meteorologists faced the challenge of trying to predict the weather. Storms and fluctuations in the atmospheric conditions occurred without warning, and scientists concluded that weather was a chaotic, nonlinear, random sequence of events. Until, that is, further study revealed the order concealed within the chaos.

the butterfly effect

This phrase refers to the idea that a butterfly's wings create changes in the atmosphere that initiate the formation of a tornado. Like the domino effect, although the force of a butterfly's wings does not become the force of the storm, the butterfly flapping its wings is the initial condition that sets the tornado in motion. Without that flapping, the particular tornado would not exist.

Incredible as it seems, the tiny turbulence created by a butterfly's wings in Tokyo can lead to a tornado in Kansas. And a person slamming a car door in Iowa can influence the weather in Brazil. Everything is connected. The weather only appeared random to meteorologists because they were unable to perceive and measure all the millions of influences that contribute to a stormy day— influences such as flapping butterflies and slamming doors.

Like weather patterns, our life, no matter how chaotic it appears, is ruled by an unseen order. Our problem, our challenge, is that the curtain limits our ability to spot all those tiny butterflies flapping into our personal lives. All the storms and tornadoes whipping through our daily existence have causes behind the curtain; we just can't see them. We observe their effects, but not the level of reality where they are caused. We experience symptoms, but are unaware of their root. We go through chaos, but cannot detect its origin because we are blind to the 99 Percent Dimension on the other side of the curtain.

In our physical world, we are in touch with only a microscopic portion of reality as we desperately search for meaning in everything and for fulfillment of our deepest desires. Some of us turn to science, some to religion, some to drugs. Some pursue wealth and power. But the void remains. We feel insignificant, helpless, unhappy, and out of control, starving for spiritual sustenance, meaning, and positive change.

Is our destiny to remain locked into the 1 Percent Realm, unaware of what is going on in the 99 Percent Reality? Are we doomed to chaos and darkness? Must the curtain remain down forever?

Not by a long shot.

the 99 percent world

A physicist had a horseshoe hanging on the door of his laboratory. His colleagues were surprised and asked whether he believed that it would bring luck to his experiments. He answered, "No, I don't believe in superstition. But I have been told that it works even if you don't believe in it."
— R. L. Weber, *A Random Walk in Science*

The familiar reality we know is the 1 Percent World in which we live, yet what lies on the other side of the curtain—the 99 Percent—is ultimately far more influential.

The 99 Percent Realm is the source of lasting fulfillment. This is the domain of Light. Whenever we experience joy from the hug of a child, when we close a business deal, when we feel successful and valued—these warm feelings flow from the 99 Percent.

nothing new under the sun

Before Thomas Edison, civilization lived pretty much in the dark compared to the 24-hour, neon-lit, fluorescent-glowing, halogen-burning world of today. But did Edison really invent something new when he developed the light bulb? Or did the information already exist?

Did Albert Einstein actually discover something new with his Theory of Relativity, or was it always there?

Did Sir Isaac Newton invent gravity?

Edison, Einstein, and Newton merely revealed something that already existed. So where was all this information hiding before these great minds uncovered it? Behind the curtain: in the 99 Percent World.

timeless symphony

Wolfgang Amadeus Mozart once said he was able to conceive entire symphonies in his mind before he wrote a single note. "Nor do I hear in my imagination the parts successively; I hear them all at once. What a delight this is! All this inventing, this producing, takes place in a pleasing, lively dream." (http://www.creativequotations.com/tqs/tq-dreams.htm) The "lively dream" that he describes is the 99 Percent Reality that transcends the laws of time and space.

Arthur I. Miller, professor of the history and philosophy of science at University College London, wrote Einstein once said that while Beethoven created his music, Mozart's "was so pure that it seemed to have been ever-present in the universe, waiting to be discovered by the master." Einstein believed much the same of physics—that beyond observations and theory lay the music of the spheres, which, he wrote, revealed a "pre-established harmony," exhibiting stunning symmetries. The laws of nature, including those of relativity theory, were waiting to be plucked out of the cosmos by someone with a sympathetic ear. (Miller, Arthur I., (January 31, 2006), *A Genius Finds Inspiration in the Music of Another*, New York Times, retrieved from http://www.nytimes.com/2006/01/31/science/31essa.html)

Einstein, Mozart, and other great minds of the past understood that another spiritual dimension was the source of their achievements. Consider, too, the case of Russian chemist Dmitry Mendeleyev, who had an unusual dream in 1869. Said Mendeleyev: "I saw in a dream a table where all the elements fell into place as required. Awakening, I immediately wrote it down on a piece of paper." (Kotz, John C. et al (2006) Atomic Electron Configurations and Chemical Periodicity (p. 133) *Chemistry and Chemical Reactivity* (6th Ed.) Thomson Brooks/Cole)

Mendeleyev's dream resulted in the periodic table of the elements we all learned in our high school chemistry classes.

The following is an excerpt from a letter written by Bill Banting, son of Canadian scientist Sir Frederick Banting, who won the Nobel Prize in the category of Physiology or Medicine in 1923 and was eventually knighted for his scientific work. (http://images.oakville.halinet.on.ca/14528/data)

> My father asked more of himself than others. Anxious to give his first year medical students a synopsis of the latest research, he thought the material for his lecture wasn't good enough. To do a better job, he took his medical journals to bed with him. Hours later, rising from a sleep, he scribbled down a brief paragraph that would lead to the discovery of insulin.

Plato spoke about the world of ideas, which he said was the origin and true source of our physical reality as well as all wisdom. Our world was merely a shadow of this hidden reality. Physicist Roger Penrose wrote in his book, *Shadows of the Mind*:

> According to Plato, mathematical concepts and mathematical truths inhabit an actual world of their own that is timeless and without physical location. Plato's world is an ideal world of perfect forms, distinct from the physical world, but in terms of which the physical world must be understood.

Dreams, visions, intuition—these are all moments of connection to the 99 Percent Realm where all information, wisdom, energy, fulfillment, and Light exist.

Plato called a connection to the 99 Percent "divine madness."

Famed 15th century philosopher Nicholas of Cusa called it "divine revelation."

Mozart doooribod it ao "a ruoh."

Twentieth century philosopher and mathematician Edmund Husserl called it "pure intuition."

Many of the leaders of the Scientific Revolution and the Age of Enlightenment, including the philosophers Henry More and Wilhelm Leibniz, studied some form of Kabbalah and were familiar with the 99 Percent Realm. You and I know it through our own experiences of connection. We call it:

"a mother's intuition,"

"sixth sense,"

"gut instinct."

Now that you have a sense of the 99 Percent World, let me share with you the challenge that it poses.

the problem

There is one ongoing obstacle in our inability to control the moments of connection to the 99 Percent Realm. Accessing this dimension of Light is accidental and haphazard at best. Looking from a historical perspective, it seems that only a few great minds in every generation were able to connect to the 99 Percent to uncover a piece of wisdom that dramatically altered the destiny of humanity. Once again, think of Banting, Einstein, Mendeleyev, Newton, Mozart, Moses, Muhammad, Jesus, and Abraham.

For most of us, prior to our learning Kabbalah or reading this book, there was no knowledge that such a blissful realm even existed. Consequently, when we did make contact with the 99 Percent—in moments of intuition, creativity, inspiration, experiencing a miracle, formulating brilliant ideas, and so on—we thought it was just good old-fashioned luck shining down upon us. It's difficult for us to imagine something we cannot see or touch, much less understand how it works.

My father, Rav Berg, describes the 99 Percent Reality as dancing on the edge of consciousness, like a tantalizing dream that cannot quite be remembered. Moments before the dreamer wakes, there is a crucial instant when only a gossamer thread connects the dreamer to the dream. The harder the dreamer pulls on that delicate strand, the more quickly the fabric of the dream unravels and disappears. As the dream fades, the dreamer must become resigned to a waking reality immensely inferior to the dream.

Imagine being able to access the 99 Percent Realm at will; if we could, we would gain the ability to control all the events in our lives. Instead of just dealing with symptoms and effects, we could discover the hidden forces behind the seemingly chaotic circumstances and maddening events that "suddenly" end our happiness, leaving our deepest desires unfulfilled. We would have the power to create order out of chaos. We could utilize the Light of the 99 Percent to vanquish any form of darkness in our lives.

Think of it this way: If you alter a branch of a tree, you change only the branch. Modify a leaf, and you change only the leaf. But if you can manipulate the genetic information inside the seed, you can affect the entire tree—branches, leaves, fruit, the whole shebang. The realm of the 99 Percent is the DNA level of reality. The seed. The root. The cause of all causes.

chasing our own shadows

Consider the following analogy. Your shadow on the sidewalk presents a severely limited version of your true self. Your shadow does not reflect the blood, bones, emotions, imagination, feelings, or desires that define you as an individual. It is merely a two-dimensional reflection of your three-dimensional reality, a 1 percent image of your 99 percent self.

Can you move someone's arm simply by touching his or her shadow on the wall? It can't be done. You must touch the source, the actual arm, the reality of the 99 Percent. Move the actual arm, and the shadow responds automatically. In other words, you must move into a higher dimension to effect change. We, however, have been conditioned to focus our efforts on the 1 Percent Realm of existence, which is akin to chasing our own shadow. It's an exercise in futility.

Here's a very simple assignment that I would like you to do right now, which might help to solidify the point. Find a piece of paper and a pencil, and then write down your top five responses to the following question:

What do you truly desire from life?

Take some time to think about it and be honest with yourself about what you *really* want. Jot your thoughts down. Now compare them to the most common answers given to this question.

Most frequent answers

- Personal fulfillment
- Peace of mind
- Relief from fear and anxiety
- Financial security
- Contentment
- Love
- Freedom
- Control
- Wisdom
- Happiness
- Health

I am certain that your list has a few things in common with this one. Please note that not one of these answers can be measured, or weighed on a scale, or held in your hands. You cannot physically locate them on any map, or reach them by specifying their coordinates. None of the things that we want most from life are of a physical nature. Nothing on our list can be found in the material 1 Percent Realm. Everything we genuinely desire is of an ethereal nature found *only* in the 99 Percent Reality.

This brings us to our Third Principle of Kabbalah:

> Principle Three:
> **Everything that a Human Being Truly Desires from Life is Spiritual Light.**

And yet what do we do throughout our life? We chase physical possessions in our pursuit of happiness. Is it any wonder we are unable to experience sustainable fulfillment?

To see how this third principle operates, let's look at something that would seem to be very tangible: money, cold hard cash. Consider an individual with a net worth of $20 million who loses $15 million overnight in a stock market crash. Compare that to a person with a net worth of $20,000 who earns $80,000 from a stock that just went through the roof. Which one goes to bed with greater peace of mind and a stronger sense of security? The one who has $5 million or the one with only a small fraction of that amount?

Although this example is simplistic, the idea here is that money does not, in and of itself, give security. There are those who have millions who feel as if they have nothing, and there are those who have nothing who feel as if they have millions. Security is not found in a bank account; it is a feeling that comes from within. This is because physical objects are not what we humans are truly seeking in life. We're really searching for the spiritual energy that pervades the 99 Percent World.

the reason for our discontent

We find ourselves unhappy, unfulfilled, sad, depressed, miserable, or anxious when our desires seem to be ignored by the universe. Usually it's some form of chaos that precipitates our unfulfilled longings: ill health; financial adversity; problems in marriage; social pressures; fears, phobias, panic attacks. All this turmoil occurs for one reason and one reason only:

We have disconnected ourselves,
knowingly or unknowingly, from the 99 Percent Realm.

However, when we learn how to reconnect to this realm, we can control the events in our life. We can eradicate the chaos that causes our unhappiness. We can turn on the Light and vanquish the darkness.

Connection with the 99 Percent Realm is the secret to lasting fulfillment in life. But it's not easy to do. In the pages that follow, I will describe in detail the tools and methods for reaching beyond our everyday life.

it makes you wonder...

Why do chaos, suffering, pain, and disease exist if there is another world of order and happiness?

Why are there two realms: the 1 Percent and the 99 Percent?

Who constructed reality this way? And for what reason?

Where do our desires spring from?

Why are our desires and the fulfillment we seek separated by some unseen curtain?

Who put up the curtain?

How did we disconnect ourselves from the 99 Percent Realm?

the taste of time

A tribesman living in the Amazon rainforest will not suddenly wake up one morning and crave a double-shot cappuccino. Desires do not spring up on their own; the flavor we seek must have been tasted before. You cannot have an intense desire to enjoy viewing *The Godfather* for the umpteenth time if you've never experienced the film before.

Given that desire springs from experience and memory, isn't it interesting that since the dawn of humanity, people have been unrelenting in their quest for happiness? No matter how many wars, diseases, famines, depressions, and natural disasters knock us off our feet, we keep picking ourselves back up again and again, single-minded in our quest for lasting peace, unending joy, and permanent pleasure.

It stands to reason that we must have experienced the 99 Percent Realm before. Somewhere in the recesses of our soul, we know it's possible to connect ourselves to this reality on a continuing basis.

memories

The various desires, urges, impulses, and cravings that pervade our thoughts have existed since before the dawn of time. Whatever longings are stirring in our heart at this very moment are in fact memories lingering in our soul, recollections ingrained in our very being. The pursuit of happiness is not only inscribed in the U.S. Constitution as an inalienable right of U.S. citizenship, it is also present in the blueprint of our universe. It is the birthright of humanity.

Remember, an old oak tree didn't just spring up out of nowhere on your front lawn. There was a hidden seed. Similarly, there is a seed of our desires, of the fulfillment we so desperately seek. We will now identify this ancient seed and discover the ultimate purpose of its "sudden" appearance on the front lawns of this world.

part two

creation, the big bang, and the nature of god

the cause of all causes

Know that before the emanations were emanated and
the created were created, the exalted and simple Light
filled the entire existence, and there was
no empty space whatsoever.
— 16th century kabbalist, Isaac Luria

For centuries, questions surrounding the origins of the universe were contemplated by rabbis, priests, scientists, shamans, philosophers, and physicists. Today, the scientific establishment tells us that some 15 billion years ago, the physical universe exploded into existence with the Big Bang. But what science does not tell us is this:

Why did the Big Bang occur in the first place?

What caused it? How does the Big Bang relate to life in the big city today? Why should we concern ourselves with something that took place 15 billion years ago when we can't figure out what went wrong 15 minutes ago?

The ancient kabbalists answered these fundamental questions in practical, down-to-earth terms by traveling back to that mysterious moment *before* the Creation of our universe.

Before discovering the greatest secrets known to humanity, there is something every student needs to understand about the secrets themselves...

wisdom as light

The wisdom that will be revealed in the pages that follow is older than time. The benefit of studying about our origin is different from the benefit gained from any other study because there is a mystical aspect to understanding the root of our existence. There is a spiritual gift that comes with grasping this understanding about our lives:

> *This long-hidden wisdom is also the substance of spiritual Light itself.*

Each time we expand or deepen our awareness we open up portals into the 99 Percent, through which positive energy fills our being. Studying the spiritual nature of reality opens our consciousness, allowing us to see and perceive things in ways we never saw or perceived them before. When we begin to grasp a new principle or idea, or internalize an aspect of wisdom, a Light is ignited in our soul. This means that life gets a little bit better and a little bit brighter. It is that simple.

The most brilliant minds in history, including Pythagoras, Plato, Newton, and Leibniz, explored this hidden wisdom, and it influenced them in profound ways. The goal of studying the mysteries of our origin is to become not just more knowledgeable, but also purer, more enlightened, and more fulfilled.

> *Do not expect or accept anything less.*

pulling back the curtain

Today, with its understanding of quantum mechanics, relativity, and other leading-edge theories, science has become a useful way to explain many principles found in the *Zohar*. One distinct difference remains, however: Science focuses on how the world works; Kabbalah examines why.

Why does the world exist as it does?

Why are we here?

Why is my life the way it is?

Have you ever stopped to ask yourself these questions when you were faced with a challenge? The answers exist behind the curtain, on the other side of reality.

Before planet Earth . . .

Before the universe . . .

Before the Big Bang . . .

Back to the Cause of all Causes . . .

Before time, there was only one reality . . .

Energy

pulling back the curtain

This infinite force of Energy reached as far as forever. It filled eternity. There was no time, space, or motion. This boundless Energy was the only reality.

the nature of this force

This infinite force of Energy had a single impulse—to:

Share endlessly;

Impart continuously;

Give ceaselessly.

Which begs the question: *Share what?*

The answer? *Itself.*

The nature of this Energy was to *share Its Essence.*

what the force is made of

The essence of this Energy was—and is—infinite fulfillment, boundless joy, and limitless enlightenment.

Everything we've ever desired—and much more—is included within it:

- Personal fulfillment
- Peace of mind
- Relief from fear and anxiety
- Financial security
- Contentment
- Love
- Freedom
- Control
- Wisdom
- Happiness
- Health

Everything positive; anything that generates fulfillment, pleasure, and passion; the opposite of chaos; the antithesis of suffering and pain—all of it was, and is, included within this boundless force of Energy.

In kabbalistic terms, this ever-expanding Energy of giving is known as the Light and also as the *First Cause.*

the power of kabbalah

two to tango

The process of giving/sharing/imparting requires two consenting parties. If there's no one to share with, how can any sharing take place?

Imagine an old lady on the corner of a busy intersection. A passerby attempts to help her cross the street safely. She politely refuses. He tries again. She still refuses; now somewhat annoyed at his insistence. Why is she annoyed? Because she has no desire to cross the street; she's merely standing at the intersection waiting for the bus to arrive.

Although our passerby wanted to help, sharing was impossible because the lady didn't have a desire to receive what he was offering: in this case, assistance crossing the street. Think about this last idea for an extra moment.

Desire must be present for giving to take place.

the vessel

In order to impart Its Essence, the Light created a receiver—in kabbalistic terms, a *Vessel*—with which to share its beneficence.

The nature of this Vessel was an infinite *Desire to Receive*. For every kind of fulfillment the Light imparted, there was a corresponding Desire to Receive that fulfillment in the Vessel.

Because the essence of the Light was an infinite variety of fulfillments, the Vessel consisted of infinite *Desires to Receive*.

In physical terms, if a box of chocolates were an aspect of the Light, a craving for chocolate would be the desire of the Vessel. If a billion dollars were part of the Light, then an enormous desire for wealth would be part of the Vessel.

Just as the Light is termed the First Cause, the Vessel is appropriately called the *First Effect.*

So we now have the infinite Light/Energy and an infinite Vessel— cause and effect, sharing and receiving. The unification of the two is pure perfection, bliss beyond our comprehension.

god and humanity

You might have considered the possibility that the Vessel is the origin of humanity—that all souls, past and present, were and are pieces of the Vessel. If so, you would be right. Just as a body is comprised of trillions of cells, the Vessel is comprised of trillions of souls.

Throughout the ages, this infinite force of Energy has been called God, Master of the Universe, Divine Creator, and many other names. Why do kabbalists refer to this Energy force by the term *the Light*?

- As sunlight expands to fill and illuminate a dark room, the Light expands and illuminates eternity.
- As a single ray of light contains all the colors of the rainbow, the Light contains all the shades of fulfillment.

The Light (or the Creator, if you will) is the source of the fulfillment we seek. All of our actions are actually a pursuit of Light (emanated from the Creator), which manifests in countless ways. The full feeling we get from rewarding friendships and careers; from personal accomplishments and a loving family life; from contentment, financial security, creativity, knowledge, wisdom, health, peace of mind, and all other forms of happiness is Light.

This Light is the Energy in the 99 Percent.

the light

Light is not God but the force that emanates from God, just as sunlight is not the fiery solar body that gives us life from 93 million miles. The Lightforce is a reflection of God's attributes and of the Spiritual Energy that radiates from His Essence. But just as we cannot touch with our hand the furnace that is our sun, the human mind cannot conceive the totality of God. It makes little sense to try to ponder the *source* of infinity, when we cannot truly grasp the *concept* of the infinite itself. However, it's enough to know that the Light will completely and absolutely satisfy any and all of our human desires.

one act of creation

The creation of the Vessel—that is, the Desire to Receive—is the only one true Creation that has ever taken place. That's it. Nothing else was created *ex nihilo*, from nothing. Things in our universe are created all the time, but this was the first Creation out of nothing, and therefore the only one true Creation.

This single act of Creation occurred *before* the origin of our universe. However, within this one act, countless complex stages or phases of Creation came into existence simultaneously. These phases have been taught through discourse, metaphor, parable, and in cryptic language. The following is an abbreviated explanation of the phases of Creation.

The Light sharing Its Essence with the Vessel led to a remarkable unity. This inexplicable unity was/is called…

the endless world

The Endless World is total perfection—the Light sharing with the Vessel, the Vessel receiving total and complete fulfillment—the ultimate manifestation of sharing and receiving, of unity, of harmony. So the trillion dollar question is...

What happened?

Where is this Endless World?

How did we end up here, in this very problematic existence?

Why are we trapped on this side of the curtain where everything is dark?

If everything was unified and perfect in the Endless World, why are we reading this book in a world that is flawed?

If we are part of the Vessel, why do we experience more pain than fulfillment?

To put it more directly:

Where is the Light, the endless joy, the permanent happiness?

I will answer this and the other questions, but before I do, I ask you to consider this:

When you fill an empty glass with hot water, the glass itself heats up and takes on the temperature of the liquid placed inside it. This is analogous to what happened in the Endless World. As the Light continued to fill the Vessel, the quality or attributes of the Light imbued and were taken on by the Vessel. The Vessel inherited the nature of its Creator—the DNA of God. This nature was the Desire to Share, to be a cause in the ongoing process of Creation.

the god gene: birth of a new desire

Because the Vessel inherited the nature of the Light, a new desire arose within the Vessel. This new desire was a longing to express the DNA of God. Specifically, the Vessel wanted:

- To be the *creator* of its own destiny;
- To *share* fulfillment;
- To be the cause not the effect.

But the Vessel could not express this newly acquired "Creator gene." It could not share because there was no one to share with. There was no opportunity to create something new and to be the cause. This one desire—to be like the Creator—remained unsatisfied. Now the Vessel no longer experienced complete fulfillment, which was a problem, since experiencing infinite fulfillment was the reason for the creation of the Vessel in the first place.

To understand what happened within the Vessel, let's take a look at an improbable story.

field of dreams

Bobby is the pitcher on his Little League baseball team. Bobby's one wish in the whole world is to pitch a ballgame that would fill his parents with pride. And the little boy does it. He throws a no-hitter and sets a record for most strikeouts in a game.

After the final out, Bobby's teammates hoist him up on their shoulders and parade him around the field. Bobby's parents are beaming with joy.

After the game, however, Bobby learns something disturbing. It seems that his father made an arrangement with both teams to throw the game for his son. His dad wanted Bobby to feel great. The entire game was fixed. From the first pitch to the last out, including the cheers from his teammates, everything was staged.

How does Bobby feel now?

What has happened to his feeling of accomplishment?

Think about it for a moment.

When one of The Kabbalah Centre's teachers first came to Los Angeles in the early 1980s, he met some teens who had just graduated from Beverly Hills High School. Their parents were enormously wealthy and had given their children everything, from the best education to their own BMWs when they turned 16. Now what did these kids have to look forward to? These highly educated teens were dealing drugs and dropping out of school; they were angry and belligerent. What happened to make these young people, who had everything, feel as if they had nothing?

bread of shame

Bread of Shame is the term for what Bobby and the Beverly Hills teens are feeling. It's an ancient term for expressing all the negative emotions that accompany unearned good fortune. A man forced to accept charity from others "eats" Bread of Shame because he has a deep-seated desire to earn the money needed to buy his own bread; he desperately longs to be in a situation where he can feed and support himself, not depend on the generosity of others. Bread of Shame has undermined his sense of his own value, of being able to contribute to this world.

In *Kabbalah for the Layman, Volume 1*, my father, the Rav, explains Bread of Shame from the perspective of the spiritual structure of the universe:

> *Since the Desire to Receive, which had been established in the Endless World, was now receiving the infinite beneficence of the Creator, there arose a feeling called "Bread of Shame." The Vessel is receiving continuously, but can do nothing in return, inasmuch as the Creator, being whole and lacking nothing, has no Desire to Receive. Thus, the Vessel feels "Bread of Shame" because it is unable to earn what it is receiving.*

> *While we can exercise our Desire to Receive for our own gratification [and] without any thought of sharing with others, the essential structure of the universe—Bread of Shame—still applies. Gratification, whether it be spiritual or physical, will still last only if there is a balance between receiving and sharing.*

71

From what we have already said regarding the evolution of the universe, it should be clear that the decision not to receive was ours and ours alone. It was taken because of the imbalance that existed, and with the sole purpose of restoring balance. If we examine our desires for the physical benefits of this world, we find that they all stem from the same root—lack of fulfillment. Whether our desire is for money, status, or possessions, the common element is always the Desire to Receive, an awareness that we have lost a fulfillment we once had. We have lost sight of the true purpose of our existence on this physical level because the Desire to Receive has become more real to us than the Light, which is the Desire to Impart.

one lack

The Vessel had its every desire fulfilled in the Endless World, with one exception: the desire to earn and be the cause of its own fulfillment.

Bread of Shame thus prevented the Vessel from experiencing absolute happiness.

This situation was certainly not the intent behind Creation.

There was only one option: Remove Bread of Shame.

the dilemma

As long as the Vessel did nothing more than passively receive, it remained unhappy. What could the Vessel do to remove its Bread of Shame? Sharing was not an option because there was nothing with which to share. There was only the Light and the Vessel, unified in the Endless World, and the Light had no Desire to Receive.

The solution?

**The Vessel
STOPPED
receiving the Light!**

resistance

The Vessel's act of pushing back the Light is an act of *Resistance*. This critically important word will come up again in various contexts, so please remember it. The moment the Vessel resisted the Light, the Light constricted itself, creating a vacuum, a single point of darkness within the Endless World. The Infinite had given birth to the finite.

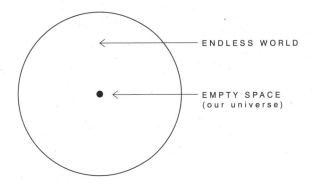

The *Zohar* describes this moment as the cataclysmic event that gave birth to time and space as we understand them, an event that still reverberates to this day.

Scientists describe this moment as *the Big Bang!*

the big bang

That the Big Bang actually occurred was confirmed by the NASA satellite COBE in 1992. Physicist Stephen Hawking called it "the scientific discovery of the century, if not of all time." Astrophysicist George Smoot said it was "like looking at God." But actually, it was more like looking at the Vessel's first effort to remove Bread of Shame.

As we've seen, science focuses on the *hows* of physical reality, whereas Kabbalah is devoted to understanding *why* the Big Bang occurred. Still, it's interesting to compare how ancient kabbalistic texts and 21st century physics describe the beginning of our universe. The similarities are meaningful.

modern science

Approximately 15 billion years ago, before the universe came into existence, there was nothing. No time. No space. The universe began in a single point. This point was surrounded by nothingness. It had no width. No depth. No length. This speck contained the whole of space, time, and matter. The point erupted in an explosion of unimaginable force, expanding at the speed of light like a bubble. This energy eventually cooled and coalesced into matter: the stars, galaxies, and planets.

kabbalah

The universe was created out of nothingness from a single point of light. This nothingness is called the Endless World. The Endless World was filled with infinite Light. The Light was then contracted to a single point, creating primordial space. Beyond this point, nothing is known. Therefore, the point is called the beginning. After the contraction, the Endless World issued forth a ray of Light. This ray of Light then expanded rapidly. All matter emanated from that point.
—16th century kabbalist Isaac Luria

According to the calculations of the *Zohar*, the Creation event took place some 15 billion years ago.

birth of a universe

Like a loving parent who stands back to allow a child to fall so the child will eventually learn to walk, the Light withdrew the moment the Vessel said, "Thanks, but no thanks. I'd like to learn to create and share some Light on my own."

When the Light withdrew Its radiance, there resulted a point of emptiness, a time and space, which gave the Vessel the opportunity to evolve its own divine nature through the act of finding Light. This microscopic point of emptiness, this newly-formed speck of space and time given to the Vessel, is our vast, star-filled, physical universe.

the puzzle
of creation
and the theory
of reactivity

the puzzle maker

There once was a kind old puzzle-maker, whose greatest pleasure came from creating enchanting picture puzzles for the children in his neighborhood. These were no ordinary puzzles. They had magical properties: When the final piece was snapped into place, beams of light would radiate from the image, filling the children with joy. All they had to do was gaze at the picture. Nothing more. For the kids, it was better than eating 10,000 chocolate chip cookies and drinking 10,000 glasses of milk.

One fine day, the puzzle-maker outdid himself. He painted his most spellbinding picture ever, using special brushes and magical paints flecked with stardust. The puzzle-maker was so excited by his creation that he decided not to carve the picture into individual puzzle pieces. Instead, he wanted the children to experience all the magic immediately.

As the puzzle-maker applied the finishing touches, a little boy walked into the shop hoping to find the latest creation. The puzzle-maker excitedly handed over his new picture. The boy's bright smile quickly disappeared. His face turned a little sad. Clearly, he was disappointed. "What's wrong?" the puzzle-maker asked. The little boy explained that putting the puzzle pieces together was the part he liked the best. The puzzle-maker understood immediately, and with as much love and care as he had put into creating the original image, the he now cut and disassembled the picture. He lovingly scattered the individual pieces in the box. And thus he gave the children what they really wanted more than anything else—the joy and accomplishment of building the magical puzzle themselves.

To provide the Vessel with the opportunity to create its own fulfillment, the Endless World was disassembled and transformed into a picture puzzle. By allowing the Vessel to reassemble the puzzle of Creation, the Light allowed us, the Vessel, to become the creators of our own fulfillment and the cause of our own joy, thus fulfilling our deepest desire and most profound need.

In addition to all these puzzle pieces one more vital element was required for the Vessel to become a creator of Light . . .

Darkness

the power of darkness

A burning candle emits no light against the backdrop of a brilliant sunlit day. The candle is worthless in this illuminated setting. But in the inky darkness of a moonless sky, even a single candle is clearly visible—and valuable. Similarly, the Vessel was incapable of creating and sharing in a realm already radiating Light. It was essential that an area of darkness come into being so that the Vessel could fully transform from a passive receiver into a being who genuinely earned and created Light and fulfillment.

So how did the Light manage to hide Its radiance?

Remember the curtain?

a ten-dimensional curtain

To conceal the blazing Light, a series of ten curtains was erected. Each successive curtain further reduced the emanation of Light, gradually transforming its brilliance into near-darkness

These ten curtains created ten distinct dimensions. In the ancient language of Aramaic, they are called the *Ten Sefirot*.

The *Ten Sefirot*

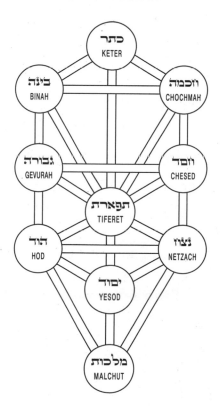

Keter, the top dimension, represents the brightest realm of Light, closest to the Endless World. *Malchut*, located at the bottom, is the darkest dimension, our physical universe. The only remnant of Light in this, our darkened universe, is a "pilot light" that sustains our existence. This pilot light is the force that gives birth to stars and souls, sustains suns, and sets everything in motion—from beating hearts to swirling galaxies to industrious anthills. This pilot light is the life force of humanity.

disassembling the puzzle

To give the Vessel the fulfillment of putting together the "puzzle," two things were needed: fragmentation, or the *space* that separates the individual pieces, and time to reassemble it. The Endless World is a realm without time and space; therefore, these elements had to be brought into being for the Vessel to become a co-creator. This occurred *automatically* when the Light was hidden by the ten curtains.

- If Light exists on one side of the curtain, darkness must be the reality on the other side.

- Likewise, if timelessness is the reality on one side of the curtain, the illusion of time is created on the other side.

- If there is perfect order on one side of the curtain, chaos exists in the other dimension.

- If there is wholeness and exquisite unity on one side of the curtain, then there is space, fragmentation, and the laws of physics on the other side.

- If endless fulfillment is the norm on one side, then there must be lack on the other.

- If God is reality and truth on one side of the curtain, then godlessness and atheism are the reality on the other side. (This means that atheists are correct in their viewpoint that there is no such thing as God—at least in this world on this side of the curtain. However, our uniquely human purpose is to transcend the 1 Percent Realm of our world and discover the higher truth of the 99 Percent, which is the subject of this book.)

Are you starting to get the picture? Welcome, then, to our world of darkness and disorder.

the deception of darkness

Although we may stumble around in the darkness and turmoil of this physical world, we can still take heart, for in reality, the Light is still here. Cover a lamp with many layers of cloth, and eventually the room becomes dark. Yet the lamp still shines as brightly as ever. What has changed is only that there is now a cloth covering the light. The Light of the Endless World works the same way. Kabbalah teaches us how to remove the layers of cloth, one curtain at a time, to bring ever more Light into our life and into the world.

adam and atom: partners in creation

In a process whose explanation lies beyond the scope of this book, the one infinite Vessel broke into two distinct forces of spiritual energy, and the male principle, called Adam, separated from the female principle, called Eve. These two segments then shattered into countless pieces, creating male and female souls. Lesser sparks created the animal kingdom, even smaller sparks formed the vegetable kingdom, and the smallest sparks became the tiniest fragments of matter and energy that make up the cosmos. So everything from atoms to zebras, from microbes to musicians, traces its beginnings to this cosmic shattering. Everything in our universe is a portion of the original Vessel.

Moreover, everyone's soul is part of the first, infinite, primordial Soul that split and shattered.

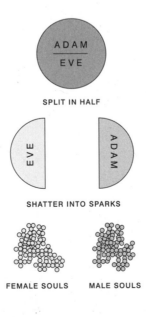

ADAM
EVE

SPLIT IN HALF

EVE   ADAM

SHATTER INTO SPARKS

FEMALE SOULS   MALE SOULS

Therefore, according to the *Zohar*, everything in the universe is imbued with its own spark of Light, its own life force. Does this mean that even inanimate objects have souls? The answer is yes. The only difference between the soul of a rock and the soul of a rock star is the degree and intensity of their desire to receive Light.

The more Light an entity desires and receives, the greater its intelligence and self-awareness. A human being is more intelligent and self-aware than an ant, and an ant is more intelligent and self-aware than a rock.

interacting souls

Because the Vessel shattered into pieces, each individual spark of soul now has others to share and interact with as it works toward its goal of creating Light.

So now you know who you really are: You are a spark of the original shattered Vessel. So is your best friend and your worst enemy. Even the plants in your garden harken back to the First Cause and the First Effect.

Now you also know that your very essence, the actual stuff that you are made of, is *desire*. You desire Light. This means you desire happiness, wisdom, fun, fulfillment, peace of mind, well-being, and a whole lot of pleasure. All these elements of Light were hidden away so that you could overcome Bread of Shame by becoming the *cause* of your own illumination.

Before we reveal how we become the actual cause of our own Light, there is one more important phase of Creation that must be mentioned because it tells us precisely where this Light is and how to· access it at will.

labor contractions

At the precise moment of the Vessel's shattering, the ten dimensions underwent a sudden contraction in preparation for the birth of our universe. Six of the ten dimensions enfolded into one, and are known collectively as the *Upper World*.

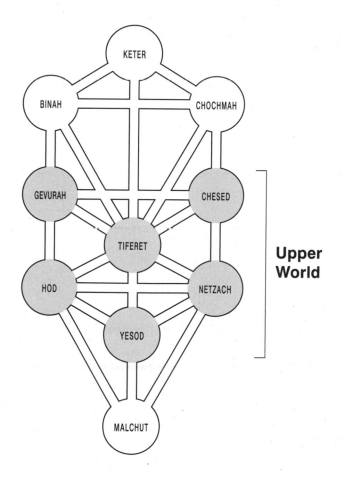

This contraction is the secret behind the phrase: *six days of Creation*. After all, shouldn't an all-powerful Creator be able to whip up a universe in less than a nanosecond! Why six days?

The phrase has nothing at all to do with the concept of time as we know it. "Six days of Creation" is code for the unification of the six dimensions into one.

science catches up with kabbalah

Two thousand years after the *Zohar* revealed that reality exists in ten dimensions—and that six of those dimensions are compacted into one—physicists arrived at the same conclusion. This is known as Superstring Theory.

According to this theory, our universe is built of tiny, vibrating, string-like loops. Different vibrations of the strings create different particles of matter. Brian Greene, one of the leading string theorists today, describes this notion in his book, *The Elegant Universe: Superstrings, Hidden Dimensions, and the Quest for the Ultimate Theory:*

> *Just as the vibrational patterns of a violin string give rise to different musical notes, the different vibrational patterns of a fundamental string give rise to different masses and force charges. String theory also requires extra space dimensions that must be curled up to a very small size to be consistent with our never having seen them.*

As it turns out, the number of dimensions required to make this theory work is ten. And what's more is that, according to scientists, the number of dimensions that are curled up and compacted into one is six. These are identical to the numbers discussed in the *Zohar*.

Dr. Michio Kaku is an internationally recognized authority in theoretical physics and a leading proponent of Superstring Theory. In his book *Hyperspace: A Scientific Odyssey Through Parallel Universes, Time Warps, and the 10th Dimension,* Dr. Kaku discusses the impact of this new—and millennia-old—idea on the scientific community. "To its supporters, this prediction that the Universe originally began in ten dimensions introduces a startling new realm of breathtaking mathematics into the world of physics," Dr. Kaku wrote. "To its critics, it borders on science fiction."

In an interview I conducted for this book, Dr. Kaku expressed his surprise by the intriguing similarities between Kabbalah and the Superstring Theory. Says Kaku:"It's eerie how the magic numbers of physics and the unified field theory are found in the Kabbalah!"

a practical science

What does all this intriguing scientific–Kabbalistic convergence mean to us on a practical level? How do the events in our lives relate to an explosion that occurred some 15 billion years ago? Why should we care if the universe has 10 dimensions, or even 50 dimensions, for that matter? What does this have to do with the stresses in our own lives? And how is this relevant to our desire for endless fulfillment?

The gift of Rav Ashlag, the founder of The Kabbalah Centre, was that he synthesized this knowledge and brought it down to a level of understanding where we could use it to achieve the purpose of life and the birthright of humanity—happiness.

The six dimensions that lie just beyond our perception are known collectively as the Upper World. The Upper World is the 99 Percent Realm that we spoke about earlier (see the illustration on page 97).

- It is this 99 Percent Realm that we touch during those rare moments of clarity, rapture, insight, expanded consciousness, epiphany, or even the revelation that allows us to pick the winning numbers in the lottery.

- When Michael Jordan sank the winning shot to win the NCAA National Championship and launch his career, the joy he experienced emanated from this realm.

- When your heart beats like a drum and something overwhelms you as you catch a glimpse of your soul mate, you're touching the 99 Percent.

- When you're on the beach with the sun caressing you and you haven't a care in the world, this serenity flows from the Upper World.

- Whenever you've felt happiness, tranquility, inner peace, and the confidence that you could conquer anything, you were touching one of the *Ten Sefirot.*

This is the realm that Plato wrote about—the timeless world of ideas or forms that exists beyond the physical world of the five senses.

In one of his theological manuscripts on display at Trinity College in Cambridge (I was honored to be given a microfilm of his actual writings as a gift), Sir Isaac Newton wrote:

> *Plato, traveling to Egypt when the Jews were numerous in that country, learnt there his metaphysical opinions about the superior beings and formal causes of all things, which he calls Ideas and which the kabbalists call Sefirot.*

When we elevate ourselves and connect to this higher world, we bring lasting positive change into our lives. Remember, when you move the arm, the shadow on the wall responds automatically. When we "move" the 99 Percent, our 1 Percent World follows suit.

How many times have we wondered, "Where's God when we need Him most?" How many times have we asked why it's so difficult to connect with the Creator? The key to connecting to the Creator is knowing *how* to connect ourselves to the Upper World known as the 99 Percent Realm.

the theory of reactivity

Everyone thinks of changing the world,
but no one thinks of changing himself.
— Leo Tolstoy

When we look into the realm of the 99 Percent, we discover four key attributes of the Light that we inherited and need to express in our world in order to remove Bread of Shame.

They are:

- Being the *cause*

- Being a *creator*

- Being in *control*

- *Sharing*

In our physical world, these four qualities merge into a single behavior. My father, Rav Berg, elegantly expresses it in one succinct phrase:

Being proactive

All the traits of the Vessel—that is, of humanity in the 1 Percent Realm—can be expressed in another word:

Reactive

Reactive means:

- Being the *effect*

- Being a *created entity*

- Being *controlled by* everything

- *Receiving*

further defining reactive behavior

The source of all reactive behavior is the Desire to Receive. This is the original desire that was created in the Endless World. Although the original Desire to Receive was for the good things that are found in the Light, our Desire to Receive on this side of the curtain is tainted by our ego and includes greed, selfishness, self-indulgence, anger, envy, and the like.

Reactive behavior is any reaction we have in response to external situations. This behavior can include resentment, jealousy, pride, low self-esteem, vindictiveness, frustration, and good old-fashioned hatred.

Take a moment and reflect upon these reactions. Recall times when you felt these emotions. Think about the situations that caused these feelings to come about. In truth, almost all of our behavior is reactive. But that is by design. Remember, our essence is the *desire to receive fulfillment*. Our consciousness is built on reactive, impulsive, instinctive desires. Rising above this consciousness constitutes genuine spiritual transformation.

Let's now examine how all these kabbalistic concepts play out in our real world.

the meaning of life

In simplest terms, the mission of the Vessel is to transform itself from a reactive force into a proactive force.

This is the ultimate purpose of life.

This is the reason for our existence.

This is the way back home.

This is the path to endless fulfillment.

This is the secret to removing Bread of Shame and expressing our godly DNA.

This is the true definition of the term *spiritual transformation.*

Here we have now unveiled the Fourth Principle of Kabbalah:

> Principle Four:
> **The Purpose of Life Is Spiritual Transformation from a Reactive Being to a Proactive Being.**

deconstructing the theory of reactivity

- When we *react* to any external situations and events in our lives, we are merely an effect and not a cause; we are reactive, not proactive.

- When we live our lives without any personal growth or change of nature, we are not *creating* new spiritual levels of existence for ourselves.

- When we allow outside forces to influence our feelings, positive or negative, we have surrendered *control*.

- When we exhibit egocentric or self-centered behavior, we are not *sharing* but instead receiving gratification for the ego.

Reflect on this before proceeding to the next page.

a spiritual big bang

Whenever we react in life, whether with anger or with pleasure, the energy we feel is a *direct* connection to the 99 Percent. This is Light the Vessel first received in the Endless World—that burst of energy, rush of pleasure, feeling of gratification. However, it was also this initial explosion of Light that gave birth to Bread of Shame.

Whenever we behave reactively, we are denying our inherited godly nature. Our soul then replays the original act of resistance and stops the Light from flowing. Consider this a spiritual version of the Big Bang. Metaphorically, another cloth is flung over the lamp. Life gets darker. And that's when the pleasure wears off. The thrill leaves us. The rush is gone. This is why we feel so down after we've reacted by exploding in anger toward our friends or spouse. This is why we crash · after experiencing a high from drugs. This is why our excitement quickly dissipates after we buy a new car or new clothes. The gratification or pleasure was not created through our own proactive efforts; instead, something external was responsible for our fulfillment.

In the same way, if someone pays us a compliment and it makes us feel better about ourselves, the *other person* is the cause and we are the effect. Our happiness will be only temporary. Our soul is forced to reprise the act of Resistance, to cut off the Light to prevent Bread of Shame. Darkness is the inevitable result.

a spiritual alternative

There is another way available to us that keeps "spiritual Big Bangs" from taking place in our life. This is the proactive use of Resistance, and it means stopping our reactive impulses *through our own choice.*

Although this strategy can be expressed in one short sentence, accomplishing it requires almost superhuman will and self-restraint. We'll find out why it's easier said than done shortly. But first, try the following exercise to deepen your understanding of Resistance and to learn what real transformation means.

the $100,000 quiz

Setting: *A hundred thousand dollars in small-denomination bills lies on top of the front desk in a business.*

Scenario Number One: *A man walks in and sees the money. He makes sure no one is watching, then scoops up the cash and flees like a bandit.*

Scenario Number Two: *A man walks in and sees the money. He begins shaking; fearing the prospect of even touching the cash, let alone stealing it. He flees the building like a scared rabbit.*

Scenario Number Three: *A man walks in and sees the money. He checks to see that no one is looking. Then he scoops up the cash and begins to flee. But he stops. He agonizes for a moment and decides to return the money to the desk.*

Scenario Number Four: *A man walks in and sees the money. He takes it and places it inside a briefcase. He locks the briefcase and hands it over to the authorities for safekeeping. He leaves a note on the desk that informs whoever has misplaced a large sum of cash to contact him, and he will direct that person to the authorities to retrieve the money.*

Which of these scenarios reveals the most spiritual Light in our world? Which person expresses the most spiritual Light in his own life? Based on what we have learned so far, let's briefly examine each scenario to discover the answer.

Scenario Number One: In this case the man is governed by his reactive, instinctive Desire to Receive, which tells him to take the money and run. Reactive behavior produces no Light.

Scenario Number Two: This man is merely reacting to his fear of even the thought of stealing the money. Reacting to his natural instinct produces no Light. The man enters the building and leaves it again with his nature unchanged.

Scenario Number Three: The man initially reacts to his desire to steal the cash, but then he stops his reaction. He shuts it down proactively. Then going against his initial instinct, he transforms his nature in this one instant and returns the money. His transformation from reactive to proactive reveals spiritual Light.

Scenario Number Four: Here the man merely reacts to his instinctive desire to do the right thing. He was already in a proactive state of mind concerning stealing the money. No change of nature occurs. He remains the same person. Such behavior produces no additional Light in this person's life.

The man in this fourth scenario can still reveal Light, however. After returning the money, he must *not* react to his ego, which is telling him how kind and virtuous he is. He must *resist* his Desire to Receive— which, in this case, means his desire to receive praise for his good deed. He must realize that for him, the great opportunity to reveal Light is not the physical act of returning the money; it lies in keeping his good deed secret and rejecting self-praise.

Always remember that our positive traits and good deeds do not automatically flip on the Light switch. The Light goes on only when we identify, uproot, and transform our reactive negative characteristics. It is the degree of change we make in our nature that determines the measure of our fulfillment.

the long supermarket line of life

The next time you find yourself stuck in a long line at an ATM machine, traffic jam, or supermarket checkout counter, resist your urge to react. Do not get frustrated. Do not become irritated and impatient. Do not get angry. The line is there to test you, to give you an opportunity not to react but to reveal Light. If you do react, the situation controls you. The situation becomes the cause and you the effect.

Always remember that the reason for not reacting to the long supermarket line, to the crazy driver who cuts you off on the interstate, or to your brother-in-law who irritates you to no end has nothing to do with being polite. Nor has it anything to do with good morals, ethics, or any other altruistic principle. It has to do with you, as in: *What's in it for you?*

it's never about morals

Historically, morals and ethics have never led to peace and unity. Morality might be noble, but it won't ever change the nature of the beast. Never has, never will. We are a species of receivers, as in: *What's in it for me?*

And that's okay. This was the Creator's intent.

To be motivated to take action, people must *receive something* in return. The purpose of Resistance is to remove Bread of Shame so that we can receive the Light we ask for and desire. So stop your reactive nature of constantly thinking about yourself—not because this is morally the right thing to do, but because the transformation will serve your best interests. It's a paradox: When you stop thinking of yourself, then the Light thinks about you, and you can receive everything, *with no fear of losing it later.*

Each of us has the power to bring fulfillment into our life by transforming our nature. Then when enough of us achieve this level of transformation, the world will be overwhelmed with an unimaginable infusion of Light.

the moment of transformation

We have two choices in life:

1. React to a situation, thus leaving ourselves in the darkness of the 1 Percent Realm.

2. Proactively resist our desire to react, thereby connecting ourselves to the 99 Percent Reality.

Being proactive, option number two removes Bread of Shame, thus clearing the way for Light to fill our life in that particular circumstance. Put another way, the instant we resist a reaction, we transform a particular aspect of our self. This transformation is the purpose of our existence. We automatically link up with the 99 Percent, and the appropriate measure of Light radiates forth.

We have now arrived at the Fifth Principle of Kabbalah:

Principle Five:
In the Moment of Our Transformation, We Make Contact with the 99 Percent Realm.

the transformation formula

Here's how we can change *re*action to *pro*action:

1. A challenge occurs.

2. We realize that our reaction—not the problem—is the real enemy.

3. We shut down our reactive system to allow the Light in.

4. Now we need to express our Light nature with a proactive action of sharing.

The moment of transformation takes place during steps three and four. This is when our soul joins with the luminous dimension of Light—the 99 Percent Realm. And our action can now come from the side of the Light not our ego.

Exercise: Applying the Transformation Formula

Consider this scenario from everyday life:

1. A CHALLENGE OCCURS
Your friend blows up at you.

2. YOUR EMOTIONAL REACTION
You are upset. Angry. Hurt.

3. YOUR BEHAVIORAL REACTION
You shout back at your friend and the two of you stop speaking.

Analyzing the Transformation Formula

1. A CHALLENGE OCCURS

Your best friend blows up at you.

2. REALIZE YOUR REACTION IS THE REAL ENEMY.

You see that your feelings of being upset and hurt, of shutting down, are your real enemy; the real enemy is not your friend.

3. SHUT DOWN YOUR REACTIVE SYSTEM, NOT YOUR FEELINGS, TO ALLOW THE LIGHT IN.

Let go of all your emotional reactions. Instead of shouting back or disconnecting and jeopardizing the relationship, just take it all in. Even if you're not to blame, let your friend vent. What matters is not who is right or wrong; what matters is your decision not to react. Bear in mind, too, that reaction is not necessarily a physical response. Externally, you can behave as though all is well, but internally, you have put up a wall separating you from your friend. Stay open. Resist the desire to cut yourself off from your friend.

4. EXPRESS YOUR PROACTIVE NATURE.

You are now in contact with the 99 Percent. The emotions you feel and your next set of actions will be rooted in the Light. Now think of how you can share with your friend. You will see a surprising positive change in the way you managed the external situation that was confronting you. Your friend will respond in a way you never dreamed possible, or an enlightening piece of information concerning your own growth will emerge.

All too often, our attention is focused on circumstances. Someone we love hurts us. A business deal falls through. We disagree with someone's opinion. Someone insults us. A colleague gets the promotion we believe we deserved. A friend stabs us in the back. Such external events trigger reactions within us all day long. Stay focused on the issue that comes up for you, not on the details of the situation. The next time this happens, instead of *reacting*, apply the formula. You'll see real miracles happen.

Over the next few days, any time you come up against a challenge or obstacle, remember these four steps and see if you can use this formula to assist you in transforming an uncomfortable and potentially chaotic situation in your life into an opportunity to reveal Light. Write down what happens. And notice the darkness in your life begin to give way to Light.

the oldest game

I'm a sports fanatic, so some of my favorite examples come from the world of sports. I believe that sports are a great metaphor for the game of life and for the nature of humanity.

Imagine 18 people gathered on a baseball diamond. All of them are superb athletes on the level of Joe DiMaggio, Babe Ruth, Sandy Koufax, and Alex Rodriguez. They are given all the equipment they need to play ball: bats, baseballs, mitts, bases, even some chewing gum (or tobacco).

But suppose they don't know the rules of the game. Suppose they have absolutely no concept of how baseball is played. What would happen if all these players were told that they were not going to be allowed to leave the field until they were ready to be World Series champs?

Imagine the chaos. The fighting, the arguing, the frustration. Some players might quit. Others might make up their own rules. Although these players are endowed with all the attributes of baseball stars, the only thing they produce is pandemonium.

This is what life is like when we don't understand how the universe works. Is it any wonder we give up, thinking that life is random and that we have no control over what happens to us? Without the rules, all we are left to do is squabble, fight, or quit. It doesn't matter how much talent we possess. Without our knowing the rules of the game, the result is chaos.

Fortunately, we have a rulebook for the game we all play. It is the *Zohar*, and it contains secret codes governing the rules of the game of life. The greatest sages of Kabbalah say that embedded within the very letters and words of the *Zohar* is Light. The *Zohar* is a bridge to the 99 Percent Reality and a powerful tool for our spiritual transformation.

According to the *Zohar*, each one of us is born into this world with enormous spiritual talent. But for most of us, this talent remains untapped because we've been playing the game without really knowing how it works. We argue, we experience frustration, we quit, and we make up our own rules each and every day. Take a closer look at the different "games" you carry with you in your head as you go about life. What does your rulebook say? What is your operating belief system, the lens through which you view the world? Maybe you created the rules as a child—if I do this, then this will be the effect— and you haven't updated the rules to accommodate everything you've learned about life since then.

It's not easy to step far enough outside this playing field we have created to gain any perspective on it and to see what is motivating our actions and decisions.

Take five minutes right now to look at some of the things you desire and see if you can discern the rules you have developed in relation to those desires. I know some people who think they want a relationship, but their underlying belief is that relationships involve getting hurt, and the people they attract and the relationships they enter are colored by this belief.

The *Zohar* gives us rules to live by, without imposing constraints on our daily experience of the world. It provides us with a set of universal spiritual laws that liberate and empower us in body and in soul. These laws are the Thirteen Principles presented throughout this book.

Now that we understand that there is a game of life complete with rulebook, the next obvious question is:

Who are we playing against?

Who is our opponent in the game of life?

counterintelligence

Why does human nature seem so oriented toward self-destructive behavior? Why do we engage in activities that are bad for us, even when we don't want to? Why is greed more tempting and fun than generosity? Why is it so easy for us to become addicted to all things harmful? Why are good habits so difficult to cultivate? It's easy to get hooked on a brand-new chocolate dessert on the very first bite, yet it's nearly impossible to become habituated to steamed zucchini, even after years of force-feeding.

Anger, fear, jealousy, laziness—all our negative and destructive behavioral traits—feel as if they possess the force of gravity. No matter how hard we try to jump ten feet in the air, we can't. Negativity seems to be built into our nature. It constantly pulls us down no matter how committed we are to breaking free. Likewise, gravitation toward good habits and positive traits never seems to take place. Instead, when it comes to all things beneficial, we appear to be governed by the force of repulsion. It's as if there is a force within us that is constantly sabotaging our efforts to change things for the better.

the game, the opponent, and the roles of space and time

the *other* voice

You know how it is: You tell yourself, with deep conviction, that the new diet and healthy lifestyle start tomorrow. But when you're confronted with tomorrow—along with a cheese pizza and a sporting event—a second voice comes out of nowhere and pipes in. This second voice convinces you to put off your lifestyle change *just one more day*. It's as though you're programmed to fail when it comes to improving the quality of your life.

We came into this world to change our nature. That's the deal that was struck in the Endless World. We, the Vessel, would no longer receive true and lasting fulfillment unless we removed Bread of Shame, unless we first transformed our receiving, reactive nature to one that was sharing and proactive. This task is extremely difficult. In fact, it's almost impossible. Why is human nature so tilted toward the negative?

Why does a reactive response feel totally effortless, and a proactive act feel practically impossible?

the opponent

Real change is so hard because, as in every game, we are faced in life by an opponent, in this case one who constantly attempts to influence and control our behavior, and subvert our best-laid plans.

We've learned that the Vessel, having inherited the DNA of God, wanted to earn Light and be the cause of its own fulfillment. One way to gain an even deeper understanding of this concept is to consider *the object of a game.*

In any athletic contest, the goal is to win. It doesn't matter if you're talking about the Los Angeles Lakers, Chicago Cubs, Miami Dolphins, New York Rangers, or a team playing in the Menomonee Falls Little League. If you ask a player what he or she is trying to accomplish, the player will tell you it's winning the game.

But is this really the goal?

Suppose there were a magic formula that allowed your team to win every single game. No matter what happened, no matter whom you played, you always won. Game after game. Season after season. The outcome was always predetermined, the victory always guaranteed.

What would that really be like? You'd quickly discover that the game had lost its appeal. Excitement would turn into boredom.

So can we really say that winning is the ultimate goal? No. What we really want from a game is risk and challenge—and that requires the possibility of losing. More than winning, it's the test of our ability that makes the game meaningful. My father, Rav Berg, tells a story that illustrates this point.

There was a man who spent his whole life robbing banks. He was a criminal genius who could easily break through the most sophisticated security systems. When he died, an angel greeted him and showed him around. The man thought, "Wow, this is a great place! There's food; there's a spa. Nice sleeping accommodations. There's everything I could ever need."

But eventually he became bored. He sought out the angel and said, "Angel, can you help me out? I'd like to rob a bank."

The angel said, "Sure. Which bank would you like to rob?"

"You see that bank over there? That's the one I want to hit."

"What time would you like to do so?"

"Three this afternoon."

"How much money would you like in the safe?"

"Two million."

"Perfect, two million dollars will be there, waiting for you. Here are the plans of the bank layout. Just walk in and take it."

The man said, "No, no, no, no. You don't understand. I want to plan this. I want to bypass the alarms and security on my own."

"You can't do that," the angel told him. "Now that you've died, things are a little different. You just tell us what you want and we provide it for you."

"But I'm the greatest bank robber the world has ever known. There is no thrill in doing it this way. What kind of racket do you have going on here in heaven?"

The angel looked at him gravely and replied: "Who said this is heaven?"

Whether you're a bank robber or a philanthropist, satisfaction comes from overcoming a challenge and thereby earning the sense of accomplishment. When we don't feel challenged or don't feel any sense of having earned something, we slip toward chaos. But when we earn, overcome, or change an aspect of ourselves for the better, we experience the heavenly energy of Light.

It is the possibility of losing against an opponent that gives fulfillment to winning.

CALGARY
PUBLIC
LIBRARY

Country Hills Library
Self Checkout
September 30, 2019 17:51

39065111010805   10/21/2019
The power of Kabbalah : 13 principles t
o overcome challenges and achieve fulfi
llment

Total   1 item(s)

You have 0 item(s) ready for pickup

---

what was missing

We had it all in the Endless World, *except for one thing*: the ability to earn, to deserve, to be the cause of the fulfillment that the Light bestowed upon us. So we rejected the Light in order to become like the Light—to become the creators of our own fulfillment.

We wanted the opportunity to play the game of Creation on our own—to risk losing, lifetime after lifetime, for that one chance to win it all and bring home the trophy, the treasure. Only then could we ever possibly know genuine feelings of accomplishment and happiness. Only then could we truly maximize our power to be proactive. Without our being tested to the max, the godlike proactive seed within us would never fully blossom.

Like spiritual athletes, we must train ourselves mentally and emotionally so that our divine nature can evolve and manifest. This training satisfies our need to earn and create Light in our life and thus to eradicate Bread of Shame.

the company

A man builds a business from scratch into a billion-dollar enterprise. After 25 years, he resigns from his position as chief executive officer and becomes chairman of the board, a position that is more honorary than hands-on.

Seeing that his daughter is blessed with talents equal to his own, the man gives her 50 percent ownership in the firm, as well as the position of CEO. But the promotion creates a problem for the young woman. Her father's blood, sweat, and tears—not her own—built the company, and although the father gave her the company out of love, admiration, and respect, the young woman feels as if she has received a handout.

The daughter obviously appreciates her father's generosity and confidence in her, but she wants to receive the leadership of the company for the right reasons. Fortunately, the company employs many thousands of people and her father has always kept his private life off-limits, so no one really knows who she is. She applies for a job in the warehouse and gets it. She works hard and earns a promotion. Later, she earns another. She continues to work extremely hard over the years, and through her own effort, determination, and business acumen, she climbs the ladder of success rung by rung, eventually becoming president and CEO.

Her father knew that at no time during his daughter's climb up the corporate ladder could he have interfered. If she had experienced any pain or setback, or even if she had been fired, the father would have had to stand back and allow his daughter to work things out for herself, no matter how painful that might have been.

Fortunately, the father had faith in his daughter. After all, he had raised her, and he knew that she was blessed with many of his own traits. And he knew that once his daughter made it to the top—on her own—she would experience the feeling of achievement and fulfillment that he had always intended for her.

In this story, the daughter is a metaphor for the Vessel, and the father is a metaphor for the Light. We, the Vessel, need to express our proactive nature to remove Bread of Shame. But to be proactive, we must first be reactive. And to be reactive, we need challenge. Indeed, to make the transformation from reactive to proactive meaningful, worthwhile, and complete, we need a powerful opponent to test us.

Who is our opponent?

internal battle

The *Zohar* describes and explains the nature of the *Opponent*, as well as the various techniques, weapons, and strategies he uses. *He* is the unseen source of the chaos in this physical world. *His* is the voice that whispers "Eat the cake now. Start the diet again on Monday." It is *he* who arouses feelings of despair, pessimism, fear, anxiety, doubt, and uncertainty. And it is *he* who stimulates overconfidence, ruthlessness, greed, jealousy, envy, anger, and vindictiveness.

It is the Opponent's voice that says, "Go for it," even when we know we shouldn't. It is the Opponent's voice that says, "Don't bother with it," even though we know we should. And worst of all, when we want to apply Resistance in our life and stop our reactive behavior, the Opponent shrewdly talks us out of it.

Examples of the Opponent's work are everywhere:

- You're driving and a passerby needs some assistance. Your initial thought is to stop and help—until the Opponent convinces you that someone else will probably take care of it. You rush off to your lunch engagement as the Opponent rationalizes your selfish behavior along the way.

- You make a commitment to save a little bit of money each month and become more fiscally responsible—but each month, the Opponent convinces you to frivolously spend it all, justifying each expense in your mind.

- You walk into a health food store and spend a ton of money on vitamins of every kind, genuinely committing yourself to a daily regimen of nutrients. Six months later, the bottles sit mostly full on your shelf. Next year, the same thing happens as you find yourself back in the health food store. This time you promise yourself it will be different—but it isn't.

- A close friend confides in you, sharing a personal secret. You promise your friend (and yourself) not to divulge it to anyone. A few days later, the Opponent nudges the words right out of your mouth while you're gossiping with someone else. You actually watch yourself spill the beans, even though you know full well you shouldn't be doing it.

- A dear friend moves into a nicer house than yours, or wears a pretty new outfit, or drives a shiny new car. You tell yourself to be happy for your friend, but envy begins to raise its ugly head and you cannot control it, though you want to. Resentment and happiness for the other person battle for control over your emotions, and you're not sure that happiness is winning.

- Every time you take out a cigarette, you read right there on the pack that smoking causes emphysema, lung cancer, and birth defects. But the Opponent pushes you to override the warning, and you find yourself saying for the one hundredth time, "Yeah, I know it's bad. But I'll quit tomorrow."

Why do we engage in such destructive behavior? Why do we make such foolish decisions, even when we fully appreciate their consequences?

an ancient adversary

Throughout history, religion, philosophy, literature, and even Hollywood have given names to the Opponent, including Lucifer, Beelzebub, Mr. Hyde, the Evil Inclination, the Dark Side, Darth Vader, the Dark Lord, the Beast, and the Wicked Witch of the West.

Whatever you choose to call it, the force of the Opponent is real. Very real. Although you cannot see this Opponent with your eyes, he is as real as the invisible atoms in the air and as ubiquitous and influential as the unseen force of gravity. In the ancient language of Aramaic, his name is *Satan*—with the accent on the second syllable (suh-TÁHN).

When we look back at the history of the word "Satan," we discover that it's an Old English term that comes from a Greek word meaning "adversary," or "our other side." This is not the man with the pitchfork and the red cape that we all imagine. No, this Satan is an aspect of ourselves. The real Opponent is already inside the gates, actively blinding and blocking us. His is the force that makes us forget to appreciate our gifts, encourages us to feel entitled, and implants unhealthy thoughts inside our mind.

In our life, the force of Satan shows up as *ego* because it is ego that activates every form of reactive behavior.

The Opponent is well equipped to succeed in his role. For one thing, he is the ultimate master magician. His deceptive talents are best summed up by a line from the clever film, *The Usual Suspects*, written by Christopher McQuarrie:

"The greatest trick the devil ever pulled was convincing
the world he didn't exist!"

satan is real

The Opponent is real, and he exists inside each of us in the form of our ego. The Opponent does such a good job of hiding himself that we have lost touch with our true self—our soul—and instead, are ruled by the whims of ego, never realizing we are being played by the Opponent. We work 24/7 to fulfill our ego's every desire, no matter how shallow or self-destructive those desires may be. These impulses stemming from the Opponent control us 99.999 percent of the time.

The Opponent has fooled us into believing that we are victims of outside forces and other people's actions. He has convinced us that our enemy is some other person instead of our own reactive nature. All the while, he hides in our blind spots and in the shadows of our minds, lurking in the dark recesses of our being so we never know he exists. He inflates our ego so we think we're brilliant and in control of our life, or he tells us we are nothing so we become too paralyzed to move forward.

Most important, he blinds us to our own godly nature so that we don't recognize our purpose in life. Think about it. How many people do we really know who look inward each day, trying to uproot their negative reactive traits? Yet that is the true purpose of our existence.

Exercise: Removing Spiritual Blockages.

The goal of this exercise is to find out where exactly we need to focus our attention in order to discover Satan's hiding spot, so that we can begin to remove the blockages to our spiritual progress.

Find comowhoro quiet to sit, then take a couple of slow, deep breaths in through your mouth and out through your nose. Think about the fact that your life has a purpose; that you're on a mission here. Your soul has brought you to this world to accomplish something very important and quite specific. There is only one thing preventing you from accomplishing your mission: your ego. Your ego is your fear, your insecurity, your doubt, your blind spot. You can't see why you keep running into the same problems over and over again because you don't recognize how your selfishness is causing other people to be upset with you, reject you, or avoid you. In order to get past your ego and beyond the superficial aspects of who you are, you need to find the courage to dig deep. When you go far beneath the surface, you'll find yourself in a place where there is no ego, where all that exists is your relationship with God.

altering our DNA

When the Opponent came into being, his appearance added another element to our natural Desire to Receive. It was as if our spiritual DNA had been altered by adding a few more letters to the human genome.

f.o.r. t.h.e. s.e.l.f. a.l.o.n.e.

Humanity was now imbued with a *Desire to Receive for the Self Alone.* This additional "selfish gene" comes from the Opponent. This is the motivating force behind the reactive nature of humankind, the root of our individualistic, impetuous, rash behavior. This is what makes our transformation from intolerant to tolerant so difficult.

The Desire to Receive for the Self Alone leaves not a morsel for anyone else. Like a black hole in deep space, this desire swallows up everything in its vicinity, so that even spiritual Light itself cannot escape its power.

fields of battle

We discover that the Universe shows evidence
of a designing or controlling Power that has something
in common with our own minds.
— Sir James Jeans, physicist

The battle against the Opponent has been going on for a long time, yet it takes place in very murky, unfamiliar terrain. This is the landscape of the human mind.

Suppose a primitive tribesman ventures out of the jungle with no knowledge of the modern world. He comes across a transistor radio playing music and looks at it in astonishment, believing that the box is the source of the music. He opens up the radio and accidentally pulls out the transistor. The music stops. This convinces him that the radio is the source. In fact, he thinks he has killed the poor little creature. Of course, we know that the source of the music is really some radio station many miles away, broadcasting over the airwaves.

Like the transistor radio, the source of our thoughts does not originate in the cells of the brain. Instead, the brain is a receiving station that picks up a signal and then rebroadcasts it into the conscious mind.

During the 1950s, brilliant neurosurgeon Wilder Penfield began extensive research into the mind–brain phenomenon. His goal was to explain how consciousness emerged from the physical matter of the brain. After 40 years of study, Penfield admitted that he had failed. In *Mystery of the Mind* (1975, Princeton University Press), a significant book detailing his decades of research, Penfield wrote:

The mind seems to act independently of the brain in the same sense that a programmer acts independently of his computer, however much he may depend upon the action of that computer for certain purposes. But who— or what—is that programmer?

the ratings war

Two cosmic broadcasting stations—the Light and the Opponent—send signals to our brains. It's a ratings battle for the audience of mind. If we could learn how to distinguish which thoughts come from the Light and which thoughts originate from the Opponent, we could reclaim control of our life.

A good starting point is this:

> *Any thought that is loud and clear and urges us to react to a situation comes from the Opponent.*

> *If a thought is barely audible, just a faint voice emanating from the recesses of our mind, it is the song of the Light. If we have a sudden flash of intuition or inspiration, this broadcast, too, originates from the 99 Percent Realm.*

These two frequencies on the airwaves of our mind express themselves in this way:

- **The Opponent's thoughts manifest as our rational, logical mind and ego.**

- **The Light's signal manifests as intuition, dreams, and a quiet, calm voice in the back of our minds.**

Many of us find that we're out of touch with our intuition. As a result, the Opponent rules the airwaves of the mind with the longest-running program of all time—reactive behavior.

The secret to taking control of our life is to cut off the Opponent's signal. When we put an end to our reactive impulses, we literally turn off his broadcast.

What's more, when we succeed at this, even for a moment, the Light's signal is now free to enter that space. Our life and our decisions become rooted in wisdom rather than ego. We make the right choices, the right thoughts come to our minds, perfect words are spoken from our lips, and proactive emotions rule over dysfunctional episodes. The best ideas come all at once. We can even see the value of an opposing argument presented by a colleague, friend, or spouse.

To prevent all this from happening, the Opponent has some time-tested strategies at his disposal.

tactics

The Opponent's sole objective is to arouse our Desire to Receive for the Self Alone so that we disconnect from the Light and the 99 Percent. As we've seen, his most effective tactic is to push our reactive button. When we react, we are consumed with negative thoughts, selfish impulses, and egocentric urges.

And thus we lose touch with our essence, our soul. Another cloth is placed over the lamp. The curtain between the 1 Percent and the 99 Percent grows heavier. There is more darkness in our lives. And from this darkness, chaos emerges.

But when we reenact the original Resistance—performed by the Vessel in the Endless World—by refusing to react, we are being proactive. We have made contact with the Light of our soul and with the 99 Percent.

However, like any worthy adversary, the Opponent returns for round two.

what's up is down, what's down is up

Rav Ashlag said that due to their limited view of the bigger picture, people generally perceive events to be the opposite of what they really are. To illustrate the point, he offered this simple thought experiment:

> *Imagine a person who has lived in total isolation since birth. He has never observed a living creature, either human or animal, in his entire life. Placed before him are a newborn calf and a newborn human baby. He observes the two. The baby obviously cannot take care of herself. She cannot crawl, let alone walk, and must be carried from place to place. She cannot communicate her needs clearly, or even feed herself. If a fire broke out near her, for instance, she would not sense the danger. Basically, the newborn human is helpless. But the newborn calf immediately assesses his environment. He knows to shrink from fire. He can feed himself. Within five minutes of birth, the calf can walk and swim.*

What conclusion would our isolated observer draw? He'd probably decide that the calf was a more advanced creature than the baby. Rav Ashlag taught that the more advanced a life form is at the beginning of its process, the less developed it will be at the end. Conversely, the less advanced the species is at the beginning of its development, the more advanced and evolved it will be by the end.

The same principle operates in all areas of life. Opportunities that look promising at the outset often turn out to be disasters—for example, a sweet romance often goes sour after reality hits—while seemingly hopeless situations—for example, ill health or a downturn in the economy—can awaken our consciousness to what is truly important in life and can thus prove to be blessings in disguise. We misjudge situations because we lack the ability to perceive both the short-term effects and the long-term outcome. We react to what we see in the moment.

Our inability to see the bigger picture is the reason why *the final outcome of any life process is exactly the opposite of how it first appears.* The Opponent tries to convince us of the reverse of this spiritual truth by inciting us to react to the present moment. He limits our ability to consider long-term consequences by igniting in us an immediate response to everything our senses report.

Then, while we are in the throes of a reaction, the Opponent goes into his arsenal and pulls out *yet another weapon.*

the weapon of time

Time is an illusion. It's an impression created, in part, by our five physical senses. In reality, "yesterday," "today," and "tomorrow" are actually enfolded into one unified whole. However, we cannot revisit the memorable moments of yesterday, and we fail to foresee the events of tomorrow. Many of us can barely cope with the present. This makes for one impressive illusion, doesn't it?

In truth, physicists have absolutely no idea what time really is, or why it even exists. Go ahead and ask them. The greatest minds of science will admit that they haven't yet figured it out. They describe time as an elastic band that can be stretched or contracted, but as for why time is part of our reality, they just don't know.

The definition of time and its purpose can be found in the *Zohar*, however.

First, what is time?

- Time is the distance between cause and effect.

- Time is the separation between action and reaction.

- Time is the space between activity and repercussion, like the divide between crime and consequence.

why time exists

Without time, we would be instantly penalized the moment we reacted. Likewise, an immediate reward would appear with each positive deed and transformation of character.

But here is the problem with this kind of "timeless" instant feedback. Animals can be taught to "behave" through *immediate response training*. A dolphin will perform a double flip for a handful of tasty fish. A poodle will stop leaving puddles on the floor if reprimanded each time there's an "accident." But it is reactive behavior—reacting to immediate external stimuli. Worse, it's blind, robotic behavior that lacks consciousness, the exact opposite of what we would expect from a free-thinking soul cut from the same cloth as the Divine.

Within time, or the gap between cause and effect, we hope to become enlightened to the senselessness of our negative reactive ways, and to recognize the rewards associated with positive, unselfish, proactive behavior. But it's up to each of us to gradually learn such lessons on our own.

free will

Our sole mission in the world is to elevate to a higher spiritual level. As we've seen, we are imbued with the feature of free will when it comes to changing our ways and ascending the spiritual ladder. And free will can *only* exist if time is injected into our existence.

The downside is that time can create the illusion that goodness goes unrewarded and evil goes unpunished, even though it's merely a delayed response on the part of the universe.

As we've seen, this "postponement effect" gives us the freedom of choice between good and evil. Keep in mind, too, that evil behavior is much more than just violence or even murder. Unkind words to a stranger who cuts you off on the highway or a demeaning look at your children can set cause-and-effect into motion as well. In fact, assassinating a person's character is every bit as bad as killing that person physically.

The sin of bloodshed is not limited to acts of physical violence. Bloodshed also refers to the blood that rushes to a person's face from shame or humiliation when he or she has been disgraced in front of others.

Any action, kind or unkind, sets in motion a chain reaction of effects.

Here's how this chain reaction works:

There is a law of cause and effect in this universe. What we put out is what we get back. Based on this law, we can assume that when we react in a negative way, there should be an immediate negative effect in our lives. The opposite also should be true: We perform an act of kindness and our wishes should come true instantly. However, time is tossed into the cause-and-effect process by the Opponent and so the outcomes of our actions are *delayed*. This way, we believe we got away with the hurtful action or that there is no reward for being good.

This distance between cause and effect prevents us from perceiving connections between events in our life. We might have planted a seed 30 years ago, but by the time it sprouts, we've forgotten all about it. Thus, a tree "suddenly" appears out of nowhere. Chaos or blessings appear to be sudden because time has separated cause from effect. But nothing in this world happens that way. Everything can be traced to some seed planted in our past.

Time creates the illusion of randomness when, in fact, there is order.

time reactive

Our five senses prevent us from seeing through the illusion of time, so we react to time's influences in other ways. Consider time-related concepts such as past, present, and future.

> **Yesterday:** All too often we find ourselves clinging to yesterday. Whether we are nostalgic or resentful, if we are living in our past, then we are its prisoners. The past is blocking feelings as well as our ability to live in the present.

> **Today:** Many of us find it tempting to run from the challenges and pressures of the present moment. So we procrastinate and thus live in denial about our current situation.

> **Tomorrow:** We are filled with anxiety or false hope about what will be. We are frightened by the unknown future, or we use it as an excuse not to deal with today. We are not sure what decision to make or what the outcomes of our choices will be. Fear or false optimism consume us and keep us from taking responsibility for our life.

All these feelings are reactions, signs that we have allowed time to control our lives.

When, however, we *resist* our reactions to time, we become time's master and effectively gain the ability to bend time. We can slow it down or speed it up, defying logic. Indeed, were it not for Einstein, the notion of time being an illusion would be flatly rejected as mysticism or science fiction.

time is one

It seems to us that the past is gone and the future is not yet here. Yet past and present are always with us. It's only the limits of our consciousness that prevent us from perceiving yesterday—and tomorrow—right now.

But how can past, present, and future all exist at once?

Let's use another thought experiment:

Imagine a 30-story building. We are now standing on the 15th floor, which represents the present moment. Floors 1 through 14 represent the increments of time that brought us to this moment. Floors 16 through 30 represent the future.

What do we currently perceive with our five senses?

Only the 15th floor.

We cannot see the floors below, and we cannot see the floors above.

Yet all the floors—that is, the past, present, and future— exist as one unified whole: the entire 30-story building. And if we could float outside the building's 15th floor and look at the building from a distance, we could see all 30 stories at once!

This is a nice abstract concept to engage the mind, but what's the lesson for our life? Who cares if time—past, present, and future—is really one? Who cares if tomorrow is here right now? We can't see tomorrow and we can't relive yesterday, so what good does this information do us?

the test of time

When we behave proactively, the Opponent uses time to sabotage our accomplishments. If we think we've been proactive but still find ourselves wondering when we'll receive Light, our adversary has won another round by plaguing us with this doubt.

If we apply Resistance in a given situation and the Opponent throws a bit of time into the process, spiritual Light coming to us might not shine immediately. The delay is an additional test to make sure our proactive response was genuine. If we react to the delay, we lose.

Just as time is the distance between crime and punishment, it is also the space between Resistance and Light.

tricks with time

It can get even trickier. Suppose a wonderful reward lies in store for someone because of a positive proactive deed he or she did ten years earlier. Now, at the precise moment of a negative action committed by this same person, the Opponent eliminates time from the cause-and-effect process of the prior positive action, and "suddenly," a reward falls into the person's lap right after the negative act has been committed. Now it appears as though this person received Light for his or her wrongful behavior. It looks as if this person got away with a crime that benefited other areas of his or her life.

The flip side is just as confusing. A person *resists* the impulse to react negatively, choosing instead to be proactive. But a negative payback is due from a prior reactive action, so chaos appears in his or her life, seemingly in response to the positive choice.

Scenarios like these create the illusion that life lacks justice and that goodness doesn't pay—all because we don't understand the nature of time and the spiritual law of cause and effect. And in the absence of this awareness, we are motivated by the moment, by the urge to immediately and constantly satisfy our reactive impulses born of ego.

time to pay the piper

Time is the reason life all too often appears maddening, chaotic, random, and totally out of control. But at some point, every one of us eats the fruit from our negative actions, whether trivial or significant. You can count on it. It could take months. Years. Decades. Even a lifetime. But the day will come.

the weapon of complacency

Spirituality, from a kabbalistic perspective, is *not* about trekking up a mountain to commune with God by meditating alongside a clear stream as the birds sing. That may make for a tranquil, peaceful, and rejuvenating experience, but it is not the purpose of our lives. Disengaging from challenges and isolating ourselves while appreciating the majesty of nature are wonderful ways to reboot, but they are *not* effective ways to achieve spiritual growth.

We came down from the mountain, so to speak, to engage with the chaos, hardship, and burden of this world so we could confront—and transform—the triggers that ignite our reactions. Each trigger gives us an opportunity to become the cause of our own fulfillment. That's how we reassemble the puzzle of Creation. As the old proverb says:

Smooth seas do not make skillful sailors.

Good character does not win us any points in life. Our wonderful traits and endearing qualities serve no practical purpose when it comes to arousing new levels of fulfillment and Light. Our positive attributes are *already* in a proactive state. It is our negative qualities that give us the opportunity to be the cause of our own transformation.

We came to this world to create positive change within ourselves and in the world around us. Positive change will *always* encounter Resistance, obstacles, and conflict. We must embrace these difficult situations. A man can live in a small town in a modest house with a white picket fence and a wonderful garden that he tends all day long. It's a good life, a tranquil life. At age 95, when he passes on peacefully in his sleep, it appears that he has led an ideal existence. But did he achieve his purpose on this planet? Was there any internal change during this man's life? Was he a different, more evolved spiritual being at age 95 than he was at 35, or 65?

My father used to tell me that some people live the equivalent of 70 years of life in one day, while others live the equivalent of only one day in 70 years. The white picket fence, early retirement, the "simple" life—all these lead to complacency. This complacency can be a powerful weapon in the hands of the Opponent, who will instill a desire for comfort and simplicity within us to prevent us from making inner change. Then, when it's too late, we'll realize that we have made no impact upon this world.

Or, even worse, we'll go to our graves without ever even knowing what we came here to do.

the weapon of space

Like time, space can also trick us into thinking that one area of our life has no relationship to other areas. If we're sharks in business, reactively feeding off co-workers or clients, the Opponent has the power to *redirect* the effects of this negativity to our family life, for instance, or to our health. By the same token, when we are deceitful to our spouse, the Opponent can have the payback show up in a loss of business.

When the Light we generate with our proactive conduct in business materializes in our personal life, the Opponent may try to keep us so preoccupied with business that we are too busy to reap the reward of a mate who truly loves us and children who are happy and healthy. When Light that was due to us does not materialize in the ways we think, we assume the system does not work.

The Opponent limits our perspective, focusing our attention on the situations that fuel our ego so we fail to appreciate the richness life offers us and the hidden blessings we receive daily.

Space also creates a place for the Opponent to live. Each time we react, we briefly sever our connection to the 99 Percent. This disconnect creates a space, a place void of Light, where the Opponent hides. This is where the Opponent creates chaos. Light and darkness cannot co-exist. The bigger the space, the greater the Opponent's presence and the more painful the chaos.

Remember the puzzle? When a puzzle is assembled, there is no space between the puzzle pieces. Space between the individual parts creates disorder—the more space, the more chaos. As simplistic as this sounds, our world and our lives are much like a puzzle. When we are unified, there is harmony and completion, but when we are separated by ideologies or differences, there is pain.

There is only *one* way to genuinely remove space: *Remove* the separation between us and the 99 Percent.

nanotechnology

Briefly, nanotechnology refers to the science of manipulating atoms and molecules. The term "nano" refers to a nanometer (nm), which translates into one billionth of a meter or one millionth of a millimeter. To put it another way, three to five atoms fit within one nanometer. We are talking about the smallest possible measurements of space.

Working to build things at this level has the potential to yield benefits such as pollution-free manufacturing, invisible computers, super-strong materials, and microscopic machines that could roam through a person's body and repair defective organs atom by atom. We see the benefits of "less space" in other areas of technology as well. As space shrinks and physical matter is reduced, technology becomes more powerful. Consider the first transatlantic telephone cable. This bulky line carried approximately 32 phone calls. You might assume that to add more callers, one could simply enlarge the cable, but this is the old way of thinking. Today, scientists recognize that less matter and less space, not more, equal more raw power. A micro-thin fiber optic cable carries 320,000 phone calls on a simple thread of light.

So how do we put an end to chaos? Simply remove the space between ourselves and others, between us and our world. The difference between a scientist and a kabbalist is that a scientist still uses physical tools—albeit tiny ones—to manipulate an atom with nanotechnology. But anything physical still concerns space; and space always includes the Opponent. A kabbalist, on the other hand, manipulates atoms with consciousness and Light. And because there is no space in the Light, there is no room for the Opponent to muck things up.

When we shut down our reactions, all space vanishes as we achieve unity with the Light in that very moment. The Opponent is homeless. All the atoms around us follow the guidance of our soul, instead of the will of our adversary. As we strengthen our consciousness with wisdom, our ultimate destiny will be total control over space, time, and matter. Consciousness is nanotechnology in its purest form. Without doubt.

the weapon of disguise

One of the Opponent's most potent weapons is the ability to confuse us.

In the course of all the mergers and acquisitions, all the takeovers, deal cutting, wealth building, promotions, job changes, spousal fights, divorces, lawsuits, bypass operations, backstabbing, gossiping, bad-mouthing, rationalizing, justifying, enabling and blaming, we think our opponents are our neighbors, our enemies, even our friends—all of whom we feel compelled to outdo with our cars, our ideas, our intellect, and our abilities.

We think our opponent is the competition, or the person at work who gets all the credit for the work we do, or the contractor who refuses to finish the job we paid him for, or the person at the DMV who keeps us waiting in line only to tell us he or she can't help us. Maybe our opponent is the whole rotten world—the whole corrupt system that has failed us and done us wrong—maybe that's why our lives are so frustrating and hard.

But it isn't so. The Opponent is a master of disguise who projects himself onto other people so you see the enemy in the other person. But you're actually playing against the Opponent—*and don't even know it.*

When someone wrongs you and you react, you lose. Even more profound is the universal truth that *you deserved to be wronged by that person* because of a negative deed you committed at some earlier point in your life. It is difficult, but try to remember this fact the next time life gongs you over the head.

This brings us to the Sixth Principle of Kabbalah.

> **Principle Six:**
> **Never—and That Means Never—Lay Blame on Other People or External Events.**

unmasking our true adversary

Here's a very powerful and practical technique to help you put this principle into practice. Whenever someone does something really rotten to you, imagine that you can actually see the Opponent whispering in that person's ear, causing all of his or her negative behavior, which, by the way, is exactly what's happening. See the person in front of you as a helpless puppet under the complete influence of the Opponent.

My father, the Rav, in his book *Education of a Kabbalist* wrote:

> "Rabbi Brandwein taught me to look at those who might hate me as simply messengers or tools of darkness. "If a person were attacking you with a stick," he would ask, "would you strike back at the stick, or at the person wielding it? It's the same with hatred. Darkness and negativity are the true forces behind all hatred, and we must concentrate every ounce of our attention on those sources, not on the messengers. In the meantime, the attacks we receive will help us achieve our personal correction. The person who attacks us will receive their payment—do not worry. Since all people have a choice whether or not to express hatred, their choice to do so is a sign that they have succumbed to the forces of darkness, and this can only diminish their own Light."

To be angry at a person who hurts you is like being angry at the stick.

Recognize the true culprit. Know that the Opponent is winning as he tries to fan the flames of hatred and conflict between you and the other person.

Exercise: Releasing Negative Feelings from the Past

I want you to take this opportunity to connect to a time when you allowed the Opponent to direct your thoughts.

Close your eyes. Sit quietly and go back in your mind to a time when you felt like a victim. See yourself in the situation. Recognize how angry you felt—how hurt, betrayed, ripped off, and abandoned. Chances are that this feeling didn't go away quickly. We all have a list of resentments that we can recall at any time. That's how vivid and present these experiences are in our minds.

Notice your attitude in that moment. Notice how defensive you'd become. Are you still stuck in this self-defeating pattern? Now ask yourself this question: *What will happen if I stay in this place of blaming?*

What will happen in your next relationship? How will you deal with the next challenging boss or the next customer who complains? How will you handle your kids when they test you? It's difficult to see clearly when you're in the thick of your reactions. When we're in the throes of blaming and complaining, we don't see the Opponent whispering in our consciousness. This is one of the most difficult things about achieving transformation: We simply don't see the Opponent in action as he works against us. But by using visualization, by focusing on the true picture, we can unmask our real adversary.

If we don't challenge our angry feelings, interpretations, judgments, or conclusions we're drawing, will our response to the next challenge in our life be any different? Is this where we want to be?

What choice do we have? *We can choose to be the cause or we can choose to remain the effect.*

Now let's turn this scenario around. How can you go from blaming to creating a wholly different situation? Remember, the first step is to pause, and to question: Wait a minute, who is the real adversary? What aspect of myself am I seeing here, and how can I transform and grow from this?

There is a short-term payoff to being the effect—you don't have to take responsibility. But the bigger downside is that nothing will ever change, and you will never experience the type of fulfillment you are seeking. Right now, you have an opportunity to identify what you need to do differently. If you don't take this opportunity, however, this blame-scenario will repeat itself over and over again until you, and only you, change it at the seed level.

How can you change the seed level?

resistance and the art of transformation

resistance and short circuits

When I speak about Light with a capital L, I am referring to the infinite Light of the Creator, the source of all fulfillment. When I speak about light with a lower case l, I am referring to sunlight or the light of a light bulb. Both *light* and *Light* can be seen at work in universal principles.

Let's look at how a light bulb works. Inside are three components:

- A positive pole (+)

- A negative pole (–)

- A filament separating the (+) from the (–)

Of the three components, the filament is the most important. Why do I say this? Because without a filament, there can be no lasting light. The filament acts as a *resistor*, pushing back the current flowing from the positive pole and preventing it from connecting directly with the negative. This resistance is the reason the light goes on. When the filament breaks, the positive current connects *directly* to the negative and the bulb short-circuits. It bursts, producing a bright, but only momentary, flash of light.

the light bulb metaphor applied to the endless world

- The negative pole in a light bulb corresponds to the Vessel.

- The positive pole corresponds to the Light.

- The filament corresponds to the Vessel's act of Resistance, which caused the Big Bang.

At the moment the Vessel resisted and stopped receiving the Light in the Endless World, it changed from a reactive to a proactive state. From that first act of Resistance were born the rules for revealing both *light* and *Light*.

the light bulb metaphor
applied to life

- The negative pole in a light bulb corresponds to our reactive desires.

- The positive pole corresponds to the fulfillment and Light we seek from life.

- The filament corresponds to our free will to choose not to react, thus passing up on direct pleasure in favor of long-term satisfaction.

Just as the resistance of the filament keeps the light burning in a bulb, resisting our reactive behavior keeps spiritual Light shining. When we fail to apply Resistance to our impulses, we create a spiritual short circuit, and a direct connection occurs between our desire (the negative pole) and Light (the positive pole). There is a momentary flash of self-indulgent connection followed by darkness—the soul has burned itself out.

a universe of resistance

The concept of revealing Light through Resistance is woven into the very fabric of our universe. When we listen to a violinist play an instrument, sound waves are created by the resistance of the bow against the strings. We hear the music when our eardrums *resist* the sound.

You've all seen those images of the Earth from space, right? Like a sparkling blue jewel, the Earth is illuminated against the blackness. This is the principle of Resistance at work. The Earth's atmosphere *resists* the sun's rays, creating light. But because the void of space provides no resistance to the sun, the result is darkness, even though the sun's rays fill our entire solar system.

We possess free will so that we can *resist* the flow of direct and immediately fulfilling energy to our desires. Free will can only be exercised when there is something to resist; this is the purpose of the Opponent and the challenges he throws our way.

The Seventh Principle of Kabbalah puts it this way:

> Principle Seven:
> **Resisting Our Reactive Impulses Creates Lasting Light.**

the power of a short circuit

Recall a moment when a light bulb burst in your home. When it short-circuited, there was a momentary intense flash of light. *Then there was darkness.*

What happened?

The filament broke.

The positive pole connected directly to the negative pole.

Poof!

A short circuit.

A burst of light.

Darkness.

Have you ever noticed how the spark of light generated by a short circuit is always far stronger and brighter than the light of the bulb when it is burning normally? Spiritual Light works the same way. Momentary pleasure invoked by reactive behavior is much more powerful and intoxicating than the ongoing pleasure of Light that is generated by Resistance. But a reactive burst of pleasure will always be followed by darkness.

These are the laws of electrical current. These are also the laws of spiritual current.

temptation

The Opponent flashes opportunities for great pleasure in front of our five senses. All too often, we accept his offer because reactive behavior is very tempting. It delivers an overwhelming burst of energy.

The *intensity* of resisted Light may not be as brilliant as the flash of a short circuit, but the illumination produced by Resistance is long-lasting.

Drugs and alcohol demonstrate the power of a short circuit. Intoxicants elevate the soul to higher levels of the spiritual atmosphere. As psychoanalyst Carl Jung pointed out, it is not by accident that alcohol is also called spirits. The problem is that drugs connect us directly to Light energy. As a result, we short-circuit. We crash. We burn. Then we burn out.

There is an important distinction between moralistic reasons for abstaining from drugs and the kabbalistic viewpoint. While it *is* our purpose in life to ascend to higher states of consciousness, drugs and alcohol are inadequate to fulfill this intention long-term. We need to find ways of achieving this higher state of consciousness permanently rather than momentarily. But the Opponent uses the power of instant gratification and instant highs to ignite our reactions. His sole purpose is to tempt us into creating short circuits so that we will eventually plunge ourselves into darkness.

crash diet

Barbara is 30 pounds overweight. She has been dieting and exercising for a couple of weeks. But then someone offers her a piece of chocolate cake, her favorite. The reactive instinct of her body is to graciously accept. But a conflict brews in Barbara's mind: Should she give up the diet for now and start again on Monday, or should she grit her teeth and stick with the program?

Barbara attempts to muster her willpower. She summons as much strength as she can while she tries to remember the passion behind her initial pledge to lose weight. She desperately wants to find that original sense of dedication toward a healthier lifestyle (and yes, she wants to fit into her old jeans again). Barbara wants to hold true to her goal of losing the weight. She knows she must resist.

Now, however, someone else is on the scene. The Opponent fills Barbara's mind with desires that are richly vivid and compelling, and Barbara finds herself slowly breaking down at the thought of licking creamy fudge off a fork. She finally succumbs to her reactive urge.

Once she has surrendered control, she might as well eat as much cake as she wants. At least, that's what the Opponent tells her. So she does eat it. And it tastes wonderful. Soon Barbara's body is enjoying the anadamide in the chocolate that induces the same kind of high that marijuana delivers. The good feelings don't stop there. The sweet taste of chocolate releases endorphins in the brain and gives a euphoric rush. The decadent delight also contains theobromine and caffeine, which give her a mental boost. Then there's phenylethylamine, also known as PEA, which increases heart rate and blood pressure, stimulates the nervous system, and can give the same tingly feelings as being in love, not to mention the sugar rush. Instant gratification!

But the story is not over yet. The rush of pleasure wears off. Barbara's blood sugar plummets. She crashes. Light from the cake has been cut off in a short circuit. Barbara is now overwhelmed by those all-too-familiar feelings of guilt, regret, depression, and disappointment.

If Barbara had resisted her reactive desire to consume the cake and had eaten an apple instead, her body and soul would have felt satiated. Not in an intense way, but in a tempered, balanced, and fulfilling way. More importantly, the feelings of accomplishment, self-worth, and fulfillment would have stayed with her.

We face challenging decisions every day in business, social situations, and family life. Do we continue reacting to all the external stimuli coming at us from every direction? Or do we stop those reactions in order to bring a bit of spiritual sanity into our lives?

For some reason, it's just not easy to resist immediate gratification. We set our mind toward the goal of not reacting, but when the time comes, we're ambushed by the fleeting pleasures of a reactive moment. As we read the ideas in this book, we get excited for the moment. The next day, however, when someone insults us, a business deal falls through, or someone speaks badly of us, we fall back into our reactive ways.

It is incredible how something we think is going to give us so much excitement can burn out so quickly. For a split second, we get that flash of incredible light, then it's dark. We think, Wow! We're going to get all this incredible stuff. We're going to get this promotion. We're going to earn more money. We're going to make it with that hot guy or hot girl. We're going to move into our dream home. We're going to get this new car. And when we do get what we *think* we want, the Light does burn brightly for a moment. But then the feeling starts to fade.

We can't take anything with us when we die. It's not our bank account, or our status, or power. If we are not good enough *without* these things, we will never be good enough *with* them. Who we are in the world is really the sum total of Light we have revealed through transformation. Once we start to understand this—and actually live this way—it is incredibly liberating.

This brings us to the Eighth Principle of Kabbalah:

> Principle Eight:
> **Reactive Behavior Creates Intense Sparks of Light, but Eventually Leaves Darkness in Its Wake.**

suppressing versus resistance

Resistance is not suppression. It does not mean I'm going to shove my feelings under the rug. For example, if my buttons get pushed, I'll get angry. I'm not going to go into denial and act as if I'm not angry. Resistance, in effect, means saying to yourself: *I know I'm so angry that I'm probably going to say something that I'll regret later, so right now I'm going to take a little time out. I'm going to hit the pause button and hold on a minute. Gather myself and ask, How do I want to handle this? I'm going to take a walk, and when I calm down, we can talk about it.*

If I come from a place of explosive rage, there's no way I will create fulfillment with my actions. It may be important to express what I'm angry about, but I need to do it when I'm not in reactive mode. I might need to be assertive, but I can do so without provoking more anger, perhaps by saying, "Listen, I need to talk to you about something. I'm upset with what you did. I would like you to understand where I'm coming from. Did I misunderstand something?"

Resistance is also not about suppressing our desires. Instead, it's about not trying to receive everything all at once. I'll give you a simple example. I love chocolate, chocolate cake in particular (as you may have gathered from many of my previous examples). But I've also come to realize that after I've had one piece of chocolate cake, it's time to put on the brakes because I'm going to have a headache if I continue eating. For now, one piece is enough. Resistance doesn't mean that I have to stop liking chocolate cake. I love it! I'm not repressing or shutting off my desire for chocolate cake, but I am choosing to limit how much I'm taking in.

We all want Light. That's one of the first universal laws. We all are driven by the desire for lasting fulfillment. But it's important to make sure we don't draw too much Light at one time. It's a bit like a sponge that becomes saturated and can't absorb any more water.

If I try to get too much attention, if I love to hear myself speak, I'm bound to cause conflict around me because people will become sick of me. I need to say to myself, "You know what? I need to apply the transformation formula here and shut down my reactive system. It's time to stop speaking." In this way, I control my need to make everything all about me. It's our nature to want to take for ourselves, yet we need to learn how to control how much we are taking in.

There is a very fine line between shutting down our reactive systems and suppressing our emotions. Suppressed emotions gather force. The pressure builds and eventually we blow.

Resistance, on the other hand, creates a momentary struggle, which is quickly followed by calm and clarity. If someone angers us and we apply resistance in an honest and authentic way, there is no animosity, no vengeance in our hearts. We do not feel insulted or hurt. If we feel those emotions, if we are still caught up in the drama of the moment, this means we have failed to recognize and seize the real opportunity/lesson. We have failed to see the Opponent challenging us to become our greater self.

Here's our clue. When we recognize that anger and other negative emotions are tests to see if we can rise to the occasion, earn our blessings, and remove Bread of Shame, we will know that we have applied Resistance. We will feel the presence of the Light that results from our transformational action.

At first, the effort we make will be a combination of suppression and authentic Resistance. That's okay. Just making an effort gradually removes layers of reactive emotions. Consistent effort at Resistance will progressively cleanse reckless behavior, selfish desires, and negative thoughts from our nature. *Certainty* that we are drawing Light and *awareness* of this process, which is part of the spiritual system, are just as important as our attempts at Resistance.

Our ability to resist reactive emotions becomes more refined as we continue to grow. We become more proficient as we experience this process and internalize these principles.

coping versus resistance

When we resist the urge to react, and thereby create a space for Light to enter our being, this spiritual energy transforms and purifies our consciousness. Merely coping, on the other hand, will not move us forward. When we apply Resistance with the awareness that we are removing Bread of Shame and growing into who we are meant to be, our actions inject Light into the seed of the problem. Knowing that we are transforming from reactive to proactive will generate Light. This Light will illuminate the unseen root cause of our anxiety, gradually eliminating fear from our life. In the dimension of Light, negativity has no part. By resisting our impulse to react, we can uproot, cleanse, and eradicate anxiety from our experience.

the joy of obstacles:
an alternative view of life's challenges

From a kabbalistic perspective, spiritual transformation means being engaged in life, confronting our chaos and our reactions to it.

To help us receive more spiritual Light in our life, we must take a new approach to our challenges, which brings us to the Ninth Principle of Kabbalah:

> Principle Nine:
> **Obstacles Are Our Opportunity to Connect to the Light.**

The more challenges we face, the more chances we have to plug into the Light. The greater the number of triggers igniting our reactions, the more we can *resist* and transform them. After all, *transforming* is the purpose of our life (see Principle Four), and only an obstacle can give us that opportunity.

when bigger is better

The Resistance we apply in a situation also determines *how much* Light we receive. Imagine a tiny stone in space. It reflects an amount of light relative to its size. Suppose we put a 50 square foot sheet of mirror in space. More reflection occurs; therefore, more Light is revealed.

This simple principle is the key to determining how much spiritual Light we each generate. The more Light we reflect, the more we receive. The more we *resist* our reactive behavior, the more happiness and pleasure radiate from our lives.

It works like this:

- The bigger the problem, the stronger our urge to react.

- The bigger the urge to react, the more Resistance we have to apply to stop it.

- The more Resistance we apply, the more spiritual Light we bring into our life and the lives of people around us.

So remember the following Tenth Principle of Kabbalah the next time a formidable challenge looms on the horizon:

> Principle Ten:
> **The Greater the Obstacle, the Greater the Potential Light.**

the path of most resistance

Most people tend to choose the path of least resistance in life. They look for the easy, comfortable situations. But staying in our comfort zone doesn't generate lasting Light. We must learn to flee our comfort zone and plunge headfirst into uncomfortable situations. That is where we can apply the most Resistance. Whatever is hardest for us to resist, that's what we need to restrict. The easy ones aren't our true battles. It is really only Resistance when we're doing something that's difficult.

True, the path of greater Resistance causes short-term pain and discomfort, but it's the only way to generate long-term fulfillment. Difficult though it may seem, we should embrace rather than avoid problems and obstacles. They are true opportunities—the quickest path to transformation, growth, and the ultimate in happiness.

the million-dollar opportunity

Suppose you're in extreme financial difficulty. God comes to you and says He will give you one million dollars every time someone hurts you or angers you—provided you completely *let go* of any reactive feelings. Simply put, you cannot take anything personally.

What would be on your mind all day?

You'd be praying for God to send you people to hurt you. You'd wake up every morning searching out difficult relationships, offensive people, and chaotic circumstances.

Here's a story that exaggerates in order to illustrate this lesson.

The Landowner and the Deputy

There was once a well-respected landowner who maintained a great deal of property on behalf of the king. His business operations ran smoothly, and his dealings were honorable. Much of his success he owed to a young man whom he employed to assist him.

Despite the trust that the landowner had in the young man, when the landowner was called away on business, he assigned his deputy to oversee the land, reminding him to take good care of the young man.

It didn't take long for the deputy to see how practical, honest, and wise the young man was. This threatened the greedy deputy, who decided to put an end to the young man's influence over the landowner. The deputy concocted a plan in which it would appear that the young man had made a critical mistake in his work. The next day, upon discovering the young man's accounting "error," the deputy had the young man lashed.

The young man went home; his wife rushed over to him. "What happened to you?" she asked. "I was lashed today for a mistake I did not make," he replied.

"Have no worries," she responded knowingly. "The moment the landowner returns, you will be compensated for the cruelty that you have endured. The landowner is a kind and generous man who will recognize his deputy's malice." His wife's response provided the young man with a measure of solace.

But the young man knew that the story of the deputy's evil ways would be difficult for the landowner to believe. Moreover, the young man's accusations could result in more whippings, or even death, if the landowner chose not to believe him.

Despite his fear, the young man remembered his wife's words and confronted the landowner, telling him of the deputy's beatings. The landowner looked into the young man's eyes, seeing in them the sincerity that he knew so well, along with new suffering and fear.

Without a moment's hesitation, the landowner asked, "How many lashes did you receive from the deputy?"

"Fifteen," replied the young man solemnly.

The landowner looked at the deputy and said, "For the pain that you inflicted, give the young man a gold coin." The deputy took out a gold coin and proffered it to the young man.

"No," said the landowner, "give him a gold coin for every lash he received from you." The deputy counted out 15 gold coins and reluctantly handed them to the young man. The young man thanked the landowner and ran home to his wife.

The door swung open, and his wife looked up to find her husband weeping and clutching something in his hand. "What happened? Why are you crying?" she asked, afraid that her encouragement might have caused her husband greater suffering.

"You were right," he explained, "the landowner compensated me generously for my suffering. He forced the deputy give to me one gold coin for every lash of his whip."

"Then why are you crying?" she asked.

"Because I only received 15 lashes."

This parable is not meant condone physical violence, rather it is a metaphor for the blessings that are available to us when we resist our reactive behavior and let our ego take the beating.

resistance at work

Here are some more situations that can help to enhance your understanding of both Resistance and the opportunities (gold coins) that are available for all of us within the difficult circumstances that are part of our life.

Resisting Ego

You're with a group of friends. Everyone is talking, showing off their expertise about a particular topic, but it's obvious to you that you know much more than they do about the subject. You feel pressure to speak and flaunt your knowledge. Resist. It's just your ego. Don't talk. Don't say a word. Recognize the spiritual opportunity. Light will enter and you may learn something valuable from the conversation.

Resisting Inverted Ego

After a business presentation, everyone is asking questions except you. You feel pressured. You're afraid of what the people in the room might be thinking about you. You become self-conscious. Your immediate reaction is to speak out of insecurity. This is *inverted* ego-thinking. Resist. Let it go. Worrying about what others think is also reactive behavior. Later, you'll probably have about a half dozen people approach you and strike up a conversation, and you will see that your insecurity was totally unwarranted.

Resisting Laziness

A thought comes to you. Totally excited about it, you are intent on acting upon it. Then procrastination sets in. You put it off. *Resist this.* Resistance doesn't necessarily mean slowing down or standing still. Often it means overcoming and resisting the desire to stop. Dive in head first. Take a risk and finish what you start.

Resisting Judgment

An argument erupts between members of your family or close friends. You hear one side of the story and are appalled. You're ready to pass judgment and choose sides. *Resist.* Let go of your emotions. Listen and hear the other side. Resist your judgmental behavior. You will discover that there are two sides to this story—indeed, to every story.

Here is a remarkable and profound universal law: Your own reactive actions, your own so-called sins, your own negative behavior, can never ever come back to judge you on their own. Your words and confessions can never inflict retribution upon you. The force we call "God" cannot judge you, either. The cosmos will never penalize you. This is a rock-solid kabbalistic principle of life. Pretty incredible, isn't it?

How, then, do we invite so much judgment into our life?

Good question.

The world is arranged so that all the people in our life, from close friends to casual acquaintances, from our dearest family members to the strangers that pass us by in the street, all these folks share sins similar to our own. Here's what happens: The reactive negative traits of others will be shown to us during the course of daily life. The moment we choose to pass judgment (rightly or wrongly) upon another individual, we have pulled the trigger on ourselves. It is these judgmental words that we speak against others that alone allow the Opponent to inflict payback upon us based on our own previous reactions. Only when we pass judgment upon another person can the Opponent pronounce a guilty verdict upon us.

Conversely, if we apply Resistance and withhold judgment, then judgment can never befall us. Imagine the possibilities. What a kind, merciful, and forgiving world we could live in if we just stopped judging others.

Make up your mind to resist all your judgments (however justified) so that you can protect yourself from your own reactive deeds.

Resisting Self-Involvement

You're confused over some important decisions and worried about their impact on your life. You deliberate, analyze, worry, fret, fuss, and stress out. *Resist the urge to agonize.* Go and do something good for someone else. Invest a little time helping others with their problems. When you get out of your own way, solutions will come to you when you least expect them.

Resisting Self-Praise

You did something really wonderful and everyone admires you for it. You are now tempted to relive the glory, replaying it over and over again in your mind. *Resist these self-serving recollections.* Think bigger. What else can you do? What's next? Move on to your next positive deed.

Resisting Evil Impulses

Things aren't going well. You're feeling a little down and a bit insecure about yourself. Then a friend calls. After a little small talk, the friend begins bad-mouthing a mutual close friend. You get sucked into the conversation. Knocking down someone else makes you feel better about yourself. Hearing about someone else's problems makes you feel better about your own. *Resist the desire to gossip and speak ill of others.* Remember, the sin of murder is not limited to inflicting physical death; it includes character assassination, so terminating the conversation or changing the subject is the equivalent of saving someone's life. This will reveal tremendous Light.

Resisting Control

You're a new writer who's just completed what you believe is a great manuscript. You show it to a friend who happens to be an editor. You're expecting high praise, but your friend criticizes it. You take the hard-hitting critique personally and begin losing your confidence. Resist. Your reaction means you believe you're the true source of this material, not the Light. True artists know they are just a channel. Moreover, *even the criticism* comes from the Light. So give up control. Trust the process and let go of your personal attachment to the work.

Resisting Guilt

You did something wrong—really wrong—so you beat yourself up pretty badly. You lay on the guilt and shame. *Resist the compulsion to self-destruct.* Let it go. Embrace the kabbalistic truth that there are two sides within each of us. Proactive and reactive. Light and darkness. The soul and the Opponent. The God-aspect of ourselves that will help us transform and the part that needs correction and transformation. Don't ignore the wrongdoing, but look at it as an opportunity. Falling spiritually and picking ourselves back up again is how we create spiritual transformation.

Resisting Expectations

You are full of expectations for your work, but they fail to materialize. You expect certain responses from friends; they let you down. You have clear ideas about the way certain people should treat you after all that you've done for them; they prove to be ungrateful. You have expectations about a long-awaited holiday; it rains every day and someone steals your credit cards. *Resist all your feelings of disappointment.* Stop being the victim. Something better is coming. Embrace the kabbalistic principle of asking the Light for what you need in life, *not for what you want.* Ultimately, you will come to see the spiritual reason for the disappointment.

Resisting a Lack of Confidence

You have to speak in public or take responsibility for a major project. Your natural reaction might be: "I can't do it. I'm not good enough. I don't want all the attention focused upon me." This is reverse ego. *Resist it.* Let go of your limited thinking. It's not about *you*. There's a bigger picture that includes other people, not just yourself. Focus on finding a way to help them get what they need and you'll find yourself succeeding effortlessly.

Resisting Selfishness

You arrive home from a busy day at work. An important business deal consumes your mind. Your children want your attention, but you are too preoccupied. You'll play with them another time; after all, you tell yourself, you are doing all this for your family. Rubbish! *Resist those self-serving reactions.* Admit to yourself that this really is all about you. The thrill of the deal. The profit and power. These are common selfish desires. Instead, give your kids your time when it's the most difficult and inconvenient.

It's also important not to get down on yourself and think you're a lousy parent when it's hard for you to focus during play. *Resist this as well.* The fact that you are conscious of what's happening and are making the effort will bring Light to the situation. Recognize that the Opponent is playing mind games with you. He's behind the whole thing, behind all your dreams of power and wealth. When the Opponent is pulling your strings, no matter how high you climb, he will make you feel like it's never enough. In your relentless and futile pursuit for this "success," your family will slip away. Resistance is the best way to keep this from happening.

Resistance is fulfillment. Light that comes from family is often hard to reveal and experience. The Opponent can make the thrill of business feel better, on the surface level, than the comforts of home—until it's too late and your children are all grown up. When, however, you apply the principle of Resistance, you will find a sense of contentment and joy that you never knew before.

Resisting Insecurity

You and a partner worked long and hard on a project. It's a smashing success. Now you're afraid of sharing too much credit. Out of your own insecurity, you try to calculate who did what. What if everyone thinks your partner was the major contributor to the project? *Resist those reactive thoughts and feelings.* Give away all the credit. That's right. Give it away. Everything. Let go completely. As you start to do this, you may think that maybe you should only resist a little bit, but not too much, because you have to practice all this stuff one step at a time. *Resist these thoughts as well.* Give *all* the credit to your partner. Remember, the Opponent will test you every step of the way. Remember, too, that praise gives pleasure for a moment, but Light is eternal. Don't trade the farm for a bit of ego-gratification.

Resisting Embarrassment

You make a big mistake. If anyone notices, you'll turn purple and die of embarrassment. You react and try to cover it up. *Resist.* Love the humiliation. Take it all in. Lower your defenses. Lower your guard. Walk through the mishap slowly and soak up as much embarrassment as possible. Make yourself vulnerable. Recognize that this is an opportunity to wipe out your ego. In the end, your ego will be subjugated, and you will see that no one even noticed your error. That's how the Light works.

Resisting the Need to Be Admired

You're out with friends and you're meeting new acquaintances. You're introduced by your friends as the smart one in your group. Now you feel pressure to respond to a difficult question, but you're not 100 percent sure of the answer. Your initial reaction is to fake it, to muddle through as best as you can. *Resist.* Just say, "I don't know." Leave it at that. Then resist those reactive thoughts that your friends might not like, admire, or look up to you anymore.

Resisting Doubts

You apply the wisdom of Kabbalah in your life. You use the principle of Resistance in a real-life situation. There are no results. Doubts flood your mind. It doesn't work, you say to yourself. *Resist these reactive thoughts.* The Opponent is merely delaying the coming of Light. Whenever you look for results, you've blown the exercise. That's the ultimate paradox. Look for results and they won't come. Give it up, and you'll get it all.

You will know the power and magic of Resistance when you experience it in real life.

But guess what?

Once you've switched from reactive to proactive, you've spiritually transformed yourself in that particular situation. You've overcome your Opponent, and removed Bread of Shame. You have now earned and are ready and able to receive the everlasting Light of fulfillment in that part of your life. You have accomplished the purpose of your existence in that specific circumstance.

But don't get too comfortable. There is still joy to be uncovered and miracles to be unleashed. The next step is to look at the rest of the reason you've come into this life.

part six

correction, slavery, and the miraculous power of certainty

the law of *tikkun*

Each of us comes into this world to correct something. It could be the baggage that we have brought with us from previous lifetimes, or situations where we have short-circuited at some point in our current life. Each time we fail to resist our reactive behavior, we have to correct our failure. This concept is called *tikkun*, which literally means "correction." *Tikkun* means that we can repair and correct any aspect of ourselves or our behavior that is reactive, selfish, or blocked. We can have a correction or *tikkun* with money, people, health, friendship, or relationships. There's an easy way to identify our personal *tikkun*: Whatever is painfully uncomfortable for us is part of our *tikkun*.

All the people in our life who really annoy us are part of our *tikkun*. If we find it difficult to say no, because we are a people pleaser, this is our *tikkun* and it needs to be corrected. If we are embarrassed to step up when we should be assertive, this is also an area where we must make correction. If we find it difficult to confront an employee or an employer, the root cause can be found within the concept of *tikkun*.

When we fail to make a correction, our *tikkun* becomes more difficult to achieve. Not only do we have to face the problem again, but it will be that much more difficult to activate Resistance. That particular reactive trait grows stronger The Opponent grows stronger, too. And these same corrections can appear again and again in our present life, as well as in future incarnations, until they are resolved.

Sometimes it's a little too easy to blame past-life behavior for our problems in this life. We usually do enough rotten reactive stuff right here in this lifetime to warrant the chaos that afflicts us.

Right now we may be blind to our *tikkun*, but at least we are aware that, unless we're saints, we have some corrections to make. This is the first step. Next we have to identify our core issues.

having our buttons pushed

Often we do a good job of hiding our *tikkun*—even from ourselves. We're too busy trying to show the world how perfect we are. So the first step in working with our *tikkun* is to begin to recognize the baggage we're carrying. To do this, we need to realize that the universe is a big mirror. We look at our world, our friends, our family, and ask, "What do we see in others that triggers us?" The answer: The traits that bother us in others are the same traits that we don't like in ourselves. The whole universe helps us by reflecting our *tikkun* back to us.

What are the things that irritate us in other people's actions and behaviors? Are we annoyed when our friends are late? They don't seem to see that it's disrespectful, and we can't believe they don't get it. Are we offended when people are rude, curt, or abrasive? Or when people take too long to tell us something? Why are they wasting our time?

Every time one of our buttons gets pushed, it is a call to pay close attention to an aspect of our personal reactivity, or *tikkun* that needs adjustment. Whatever pushes our buttons is something we need to change in ourselves. The universe is working in collaboration with us so that we can transform and move to our next level of our spiritual development. Without this process, we'd be living in a fantasy of denial in which everything was perfectly arranged and flowing beautifully. But if that were the case, then why did we come into this physical world in the first place? You know the answer by now: There has to be something we're here to correct, or we wouldn't be here.

searching for our *tikkun*

Having our buttons pushed is one way to discover those traits that we need to correct. Another way that we can glimpse our *tikkun* is by looking for repetitive patterns that limit or block us. It's like the movie *Groundhog Day*, in which exactly the same things happen day after day after day. Bill Murray's character keeps tripping over the same sidewalk, stepping in the same puddle—until he has a change in consciousness, which leads to a change in his actions. Then and only then does his life move forward again.

We all have habits and patterns, and we need to recognize them as such or we will never change. We have to look for patterns in our life that do not bring us joy. Do you tend to have the same type of dead-end relationships? Do you have a pattern of pushing people away? Do you always choose partners who are emotionally unavailable?

One thing will always be true of people whose *tikkun* is to see themselves as victims. They will sabotage themselves over and over again. If they're starting to become successful in some area of life, they will screw up at some point to avoid the possibility of future disappointment. They'll sabotage a relationship by cheating on their partner or by convincing the other person that they don't deserve them. They'll sabotage a job opportunity by blowing the deal, or by not showing up at work, or by being flaky. The manifestation of self-sabotage changes, but the underlying pattern is still the same.

It's amazing how we think that we're all pretty smart, savvy, accomplished people. Yet often, it's only after we go through a crisis that we start to really see our own patterns of behavior. Indeed, few people choose a spiritual path or engage in serious self-analysis when everything is going smoothly.

When it comes to *tikkun*, we're dealing with an onion. There are many layers to peel away before getting to the core, and this takes time and effort. But if we're constantly judging others instead of looking at our own negative qualities, we'll keep feeding our ego and living in denial. While we're living these negative patterns, it's difficult to find our core issues, without working hard to see them.

It's important to know that there may come a time when the same trigger that may have upset us for years no longer generates the same response. People will always gossip or be negative. They will always complain. But once we develop enough resilience and certainty in who we are and what we're doing, then when these people come along, their behavior will no longer affect us the same way. They haven't changed, but our response to them has. This is an indication that in one way or another, we have worked through and corrected that particular aspect of our *tikkun*.

These core issues and challenges will come up again and again until we have corrected them. A student once asked me, "Is it worth all of this effort to change myself? I do all this work and then, maybe 50 years from now on my death bed, I'll get the fulfillment I've earned." He was overlooking an important point. The process is the fulfillment. It's not about waiting 50 years before getting our reward. As we remove layers, we are revealing more and more Light. The relief and fulfillment happen as we strip those layers away.

We may be looking for our core issues, but even before we find them, we reap the fulfillment that comes with the process itself. As we've seen, if we're on a path of reactivity and ego, we're heading into the darkness. But if we start on the path toward the Light, It will meet us before we reach our destination. Move toward the Light, and the Light moves toward us.

We're not going to find our core issues right away—that's the nature of *tikkun*. But the hunt itself is rich with rewards. And behind the *tikkun*, behind the ego and chaos, Light is waiting to be revealed.

Exercise: Uncovering Your *Tikkun*

Asking yourself the following questions may help you to uncover your own *tikkun*.

1. *Where does my tikkun show up?*
   What are my negative traits? Where do I need to make my correction? Am I lazy? Do I procrastinate? How do I get annoyed? Do I have a temper? Do I have issues communicating? When I get stressed out, am I impatient? Am I judgmental, critical?

2. *What is it that bothers me about others?*
   What is it that pushes my buttons? Is it when people let me down or disappoint me? Is it when people are rude, abrasive, and inconsiderate? When I am unappreciated? Is it when my friends or relatives yell or argue?

   Learn to identify your buttons. These are the qualities you don't like in others and need to correct in yourself.

3. *How am I getting stuck in my 1 Percent Reality, my five senses, my intellect, and my ego?*
   How can I identify the ways I'm getting stuck? Are there patterns in my life, or do I have certain habits that prevent me from experiencing joy and fulfillment? Be vigilant in your attempt to uncover these patterns and habits. Ask your friends. Keep track of what you find by writing it down in your journal.

One of the things we can do if we're not sure what we're here to fix is to ask. Ask a friend or partner, someone you trust: "Do you see a pattern where I repeatedly tend to get in my own way?"

In this work, however, we have to be willing to look for what we cannot see easily—the hidden aspects of our ego at the seed level, which we came into this world in this lifetime to correct.

Having discovered the importance of uncovering the work we came here to do, it's time to expose another weapon in the Opponent's arsenal.

the faustian pact

Whenever things start going really well, it becomes all too easy to fall into the trap of believing that the good times will never end. We become arrogant. We believe we are infallible.

Light comes from two sources—the Creator and the Opponent. Remember, the Light of the Creator is an eternal flame, while the Light of the Opponent is the bright flash from a stick of dynamite. When we strive for success with reactive behavior, our success comes from the Opponent. The more reactive we are, the more success we generate—but at a price. Never before in history have the effects of our immediate and selfish desire for "success at any cost" been more evident. Madoff has become a verb. The BP oil spill in the Gulf is now considered the worst man-created environmental disaster in history. Our ego lets us think we are riding on the wave of success, convincing us that we are infallible—until the wave comes tumbling down.

From a kabbalistic perspective, the Faustian myth of selling one's soul to the Devil is very close to the truth. The Faustian principle is at work almost every day. Be reactive and the Opponent will give you flashes of Light. When Light is taken away, the Opponent still gets to keep the Light of the Creator. And you? *You* get to keep the chaos after the dynamite blows.

The Opponent will appear to pay us well for a while, just to keep us in a reactive state of mind. In other words, he gives us a stick of dynamite with an extra-long fuse (time), so that the illusion of success and Light lasts longer.

When we are flying high, we believe that we are the brilliant orchestrators of our own success. Our ego is inflated to the size of the Goodyear blimp and is just as full of hot air. And then, when we least expect it, it deflates.

slavery

Thanks to Cecil B. DeMille, many people are familiar with the biblical story of the Exodus, also known as the story of the Ten Commandments. But most of us are not familiar with the hidden spiritual significance of this story and its relevance in our own life.

The story of Exodus tells us that the Israelites were kept in bondage in Egypt for 400 years. They were slaves and children of slaves, held captive by a series of hardhearted Pharaohs, rulers of Egypt. Then along came a great leader by the name of Moses, who, on a mission from God, won the freedom of his people. Moses then led the former slaves on a long and arduous journey, which included the famous detour through the Red Sea, and brought the Israelites to Mount Sinai for a date with destiny.

But here's the interesting part. After their salvation from Egypt, the Israelites were tasting freedom for the first time in centuries. Yet they still complained, whined, and grumbled the moment they got a little hot and sticky in the desert. They actually begged Moses to take them back to Egypt, back into slavery.

The *Zohar* explains that this entire story is written in code. "Egypt" is a code word for our existence in this physical world. "Pharaoh" is a code word for the human ego and humanity's incessantly reactive, self-seeking, intolerant nature. Thus, any aspect of our nature that controls us is termed "Pharaoh," including:

- Fear

- Anger

- Competitiveness

- Insecurity

- Low self-esteem

- Selfishness

- Envy

- Anxiety

- Impatience

- Intolerance

All these emotions are born of ego, and they control and imprison us. They are the ball and chain that keeps us from moving forward. They are the handcuffs that constrain us, the iron bars that trap us, and the whips that torment us. This is the oldest master–slave relationship in Creation, and it takes many forms:

> We're imprisoned by the ego-based aspects of our material existence—cars, clothes, luxury homes, prestige, power, and position.

> We're held in bondage by our reactive whims and egocentric desires.

> We're held captive by our fears and doubts.

> We're prisoners to other people's perceptions of us.

We're incarcerated by our own desperate need for other people's acceptance.

We're hostages to a constant need to outdo our friends and colleagues.

Some of us are trapped in our jobs or careers.

Others are bound and gagged inside our marriages or relationships.

All of us are enslaved to the physical world around us.

But with the awareness that we are still imprisoned in Egypt—still enslaved to our ego—we can grasp the key that unlocks the chains and grants us the greatest freedom a human being can ever know:

The power of Certainty

the certainty principle

Fleeing the Egyptians, the Israelites were trapped on the banks of the Red Sea. Pharaoh and his army raced toward them, bent on their total annihilation. Then the Red Sea parted, producing two walls of water that reached to the sky, and at their base was land, a path for the Israelites to cross to freedom. According to the Zohar, all the waters of the Earth split and rose toward the heavens.

As Pharaoh and his army were charging toward the Israelites, Moses cried out to God for help. The Zohar explains that God replied with a mysterious question: "Why are you calling to Me?" Concealed in this question is a profound spiritual truth: It was not God Who parted the Red Sea on behalf of the Israelites.

But if the almighty Creator did not part the waters, who did?

We find the answer to this question whenever we face a major difficulty in our life. For example, millennia after the Red Sea incident, a crisis took place in a small business in America owned by a student of The Kabbalah Centre. It was not the life-or-death situation the Israelites faced at the Red Sea, although it definitely seemed like one to this student. The names have been changed, but this story is true.

Michael owned a small direct-sales business with offices in various cities in North America. After one of the best fourth-quarter sales periods in his company's history, Michael headed off to Miami with his wife and children for a ten-day holiday.

On Michael's first day back from vacation, his accountant walked into his office. With obvious discomfort, the accountant explained that one of the company's sales managers who had claimed substantial sales during the last three weeks of December, had never put the money into the company's bank account. Even worse, this was their best sales manager with the best-performing office in the organization.

"How much are we short?" Michael asked.

His accountant swallowed hard and told him, "$105,000."

Michael poured himself a glass of water and took a small sip. As he now remembers it: "At that moment, I had a serious choice to make, and I had to make it fast. I could practice what I learned in my Kabbalah classes, or I could throw it all out the window because of the large amount of money at stake. It was up to me."

A great deal of time has passed since the parting of the Red Sea, but it was the knowledge of Kabbalah that enabled both the ancient Israelites and a modern businessman to discover the startling solution to their predicaments.

Michael had a decision to make at that moment. Should he react with fear, panic, and anger? Or should he call upon what he'd learned in his studies of Kabbalah—including the hidden lesson of the parting of the Red Sea—and choose the proactive alternative?

Here's what Michael had learned from the story of the Israelites as they stood on the brink of destruction. The Israelites did escape. And, yes, the Red Sea did part. *But God didn't do it.* When God asked

Moses why he was calling upon Him, God was implying that Moses and the Israelites had the power to part the Red Sea on their own. God was revealing one of the spiritual laws of life: *Overcome your own reactive nature and the heavens will help you overcome the laws of Mother Nature, for the two are intimately connected.*

Doing this requires *total Certainty,* and that is the encoded meaning of the story of the Red Sea. The Israelites were forced to step into the waters of the sea and proceed with total Certainty before a drop of water began to move aside. They were required to resist the uncertainty ingrained in their nature.

In fact, the *Zohar* tells us that the Red Sea did not part until the waters had reached the nostrils of the Israelites. Only then, with the waters about to rush into their noses, did the Israelites relinquish control and demonstrate Certainty in a positive outcome. They put their lives into the hands of the Light. A split second later, they were breathing easily as the waters parted and rose toward the heavens.

Michael was also on the verge of drowning. He looked at his accountant and said, "The manager never stole the money. The money is not missing."

Then he added, "You can never lose something that is truly yours, nor gain something that is not. The money will show up. If it doesn't, it was never mine to begin with."

Michael was injecting proactivity into the situation. He would not react to *either* outcome. That was the key. He was certain that, whatever the outcome, it would be the best one for his spiritual understanding and growth.

His accountant was also certain—he was sure that Michael had gone off the deep end.

"So am I supposed to just stand here and do nothing?" the accountant cried. "Shouldn't we start an investigation? We are trying to run a company here!"

The accountant was completely locked into his belief that the money had been stolen. It took Michael an hour to convince him to be open to another possibility.

"First," Michael said, "I want you to accept the possibility that the money is not missing. Second, if it is missing, that in a larger sense it was never ours. We would have lost it in another deal, or our profits would be lower next year by the same amount. In other words, whatever happens, it is correct. We must have certainty that the outcome will be the best thing for the company from a spiritual perspective. Once you have achieved that, then go on about your business as you normally would."

Although the accountant did not fully understand what Michael was talking about, he did come back the next morning with the news that $88,000 had turned up in a bank in Winnipeg, Canada.

"We found the checks," the accountant explained. "But the cash is still missing."

Calmly, Michael replied, "The cash will also turn up. No one can take what is rightfully ours. And if it doesn't show up, it was not ours to begin with."

Michael was again making a proactive attempt not to be a slave, nor to be under the control of any outcome, positive or negative. As it turned out, the manager had indeed intended to steal the money. But by the time he reached Florida a couple of days later, he had had a change of heart. He actually called Michael on the phone and confessed.

"There's no doubt in my mind that the kabbalistic principle of Certainty played a major role in what happened," Michael said later. "Before studying Kabbalah, I would have sent two guys with baseball bats to hunt the thief down. They probably would have never found him, and I'd still be out over $100,000. My blood pressure would have skyrocketed, and I'd be living a life filled with feelings of revenge, victimization, and negativity. Thankfully, I'm free of all that."

According to many spiritual teachings, Kabbalah included, consciousness creates our reality. What we desire is what we receive. If we are uncertain, we receive the energy of uncertainty. If we respond to crises with worry and negative thinking, we increase the likelihood of a painful outcome. But we can also put an end to our doubts and replace them with Certainty, *if that is what we desire*. We can disrupt the Opponent's agenda and replace it with miracles.

miracle making

In a letter to my father, his teacher, Rav Brandwein, explained this principle.

It is written in the Holy *Zohar* (*Beshalach*, 180):

> *The prayer that people pray and cry out to the Creator, especially in times of trouble, Heaven forbid, is part of the spiritual ways of nature in order to hasten salvation and help in time of distress. But for a miracle above the laws of nature, self-sacrifice is required. This is what the Creator meant when He said to Moses, "Why do you cry out to Me?"*

> *Since a miracle [Splitting of the Red Sea] beyond the way of physical nature has to be revealed to the children of Israel. Hence [God's command to Moses]: "Speak to the children of Israel, that they should move forward," that they show self-sacrifice Below. And then the Higher Level, which rearranges all the [natural] systems and makes the seas into dry land, will awaken and "He shall turn the wilderness into a pool of water, and dry ground into water springs," (Psalms 107:35) and will hasten salvation for His people, not according to the laws [lit. ways] of nature.*

If you want to see real miracles occur, try shutting down thoughts of uncertainty when seemingly insurmountable obstacles confront you. Start focusing on removing Bread of Shame and shift your focus away from results and outcomes. Remember, we *already have the results in the Endless World*. Michael already had the joy in the Endless World that came from $100,000 in his pocket. What Michael did *not* have in the Endless World, however, was the ability to be proactive and unleash his God gene; he gained that opportunity in *this* world when the money disappeared and he did not react.

Once Michael seized this opportunity to remove Bread of Shame and transform from reactive to proactive, he accomplished the original objective of the Vessel: to become the cause of his own fulfillment as opposed to being an effect, to create something new—a proactive consciousness instead of reactive one.

Once Michael had achieved this feat, Light could flow freely. The money was free to return because Michael had realized the purpose of Creation. If Michael had reacted, he would have missed the opportunity, and the money might have vanished for good. He also would have been forced to confront a similar challenge/opportunity again at some point in the future because there was still a *tikkun*, a transformation waiting to take place in his life.

To help maintain a proactive state of mind in difficult situations, we have the Eleventh Principle of Kabbalah:

> Principle Eleven:
> **When Challenges Appear Overwhelming, Inject Certainty. The Light is Always There.**

Injecting Certainty into a situation does not mean we always get the result we want. Certainty simply means knowing that the Light's unseen hand is in the game with us. There may be times when we are behind on the scoreboard, but ultimately we can't lose.

Remember that adversity in any situation is a truly positive element. Just as the antidote to a poisonous snakebite is contained in the snake's venom, the Light is contained within the obstacles of life.

We must also remember, however, that Certainty does not mean that we get what we *want*, but rather that we get what we *need* in our life to further our transformation and finally win this game of life. It's having certainty in *whatever* outcome is placed before us. It's having certainty that our proactive response is what is important and nothing else. Not results. Not outcomes. It's accepting responsibility for the negativity that strikes in our lives. It's recognizing that rotten stuff happens because we've planted a negative seed at some point in our past. It's not a matter of blame; that's just the way it works. When we overcome our uncertainty, we create blessings and miracles both in our own life and for the world.

winning the game of life

the art of becoming god

So far, we have learned that in the Endless World every conceivable form of fulfillment existed (and exists). This includes the fulfillment we receive from music, art, architecture, money, movies, games, business, stories, eating, and every other human endeavor. All of this fulfillment was originally given to us for free.

But the God-gene in our soul impelled us to want to become creators of our own fulfillment.

This is the underlying reason why in our world:

Writers love to write,

singers love to sing,

inventors love to invent,

scientists love to discover,

architects love to design,

builders love to build,

tailors love to sew,

businessmen love to make deals,

musicians love to compose.

These are some of the many expressions of a human being becoming like the Creator. All the inventions, songs, poems, stories, discoveries, and infinite wisdom of life were *already* contained in the Endless World. But we said to God, *"Hide it."*

So all Light was veiled behind a curtain, and now we search for it again in our own life. When we rediscover it, we express the spark of godliness in our soul, and in that one moment, we achieve the purpose of life. But as we have discovered, there is a big *if.*

If we fall under the *very persuasive illusion* that we ourselves are the sole creators of our success, and *if* we achieve all these forms of fulfillment through our ego (face it, we all do this most of the time), then all the Light we've created *goes to the Opponent.*

Sure, we get a quick shot of pleasure that intoxicates our ego, but then we are left in the dark. And the Opponent is now that much stronger. We wind up stricken with anxiety, strung out on drugs, plagued with chronic insecurity. Perhaps we become dysfunctional parents. Or we become disconnected spouses, and our marriages fall apart, or become passionless and tiresome. Our achievements are never enough. We still feel empty.

However, when we conquer our ego and stop all our reactions, we become proactive, just like God, and success and joy are now earned, limitless, and unconditional, Best of all, they're profoundly (and lastingly) satisfying.

This is how the game of life operates.

questions about this game

Many centuries have passed, and it seems that the Opponent continues his winning streak, season after season. Uncertainty and doubt have been recurring plagues throughout the millennia. The world has constantly been focused on results, not Resistance, in the pursuit of happiness. Accordingly, instead of basking in Light, the world has floundered in darkness.

What does the *Zohar* say about how this game of life finally ends?

Keep in mind that when the game of life is over, it does not mean the end of civilization. It means the end of death, pain, and suffering. It's the demise of the Opponent. It means humanity wins, and we achieve world peace and permanent fulfillment beyond anything we can currently imagine or conceive.

So how do we apply all of the principles of Kabbalah learned thus far to the world at large?

the final innings

I never give them hell. I just tell the truth
and they think it is hell.
— Harry S. Truman

According to the *Zohar*, the lunar calendar year of 5760 marked an unprecedented new era of human existence. The *Zohar* describes this new era with two words: *Woe* and *Blessed*. The year 5760 corresponds to the year 2001 of the Gregorian calendar.

> *Woe to he who is present at that time, and blessed is the portion of he who is present AND WILL BE ABLE TO attend at that time. Woe to he who is present at that time, because when the Holy One, blessed be He, comes to visit. He will contemplate the actions of each and every one, and no righteous person will be found, as is written: "And I looked and there was none to help." (Isaiah 63:5) And how many troubles upon troubles will there be.*
>
> *Happy is he who is present, because he who is present at that time with Certainty, will merit that light of joy of the King. In relation to that time, it is written: "And I will refine them as silver is refined, and will try them as gold is tried." (Zechariah 13:9)*
>
> – *Zohar, Shemot* 15:96-97

Woe refers to a time of great upheaval, terror, and pain, affecting us both personally and globally. Throughout this era of torment, the ego will be eradicated from our nature. Intense pressure will finally break the resolve of the Opponent, and we will at last recognize the value and wisdom associated with Resistance, with consciousness. Treating others with dignity will become a requirement of survival.

This is the fifth printing of the book *Power of Kabbalah*. When I first wrote the book in 2001, I included the following examples of the devastation that the *Zohar* predicted would befall us. Today, in 2011, we know that what the kabbalists foresaw was devastatingly accurate.

According to the kabbalists, during this time of woe, our immune systems will come under attack. Diseases, new and old strains, will torment us. Globally, there will be wars, acts of terror, the destruction of the environment, the ruin of our drinking water, and other calamities affecting all humanity.

Through these various global and personal tragedies, we will come to realize that the treasures procured through the ego are phantasmagorical and fleeting, and come at a very high cost.

Humankind will finally pull together when the world around us is tragically ripped apart. We will finally realize the only enemy out there is the Opponent, and not any human being or nation.

end of days

While the *Zohar*'s account seems to be coming true to an uncanny degree, I myself am not too fond of spiritual prophecy or predictions. The fact is, the world is hurting right now. And the world has experienced a whole lot of hurt, pain, and suffering in *every* generation. What *does* excite me about the words of the *Zohar* is that they also tell us how to stop all the hurt and how to change our future for the better. Which leads us to the *Zohar*'s explanation of *Blessed*.

the blessed

"Blessed" refers to a time of peace, tranquility, enlightenment, and eternal fulfillment. Disease will be a thing of the past. Chaos will no longer exist. Joy will be everywhere. And having completed his job, the Angel of Death, the Opponent, will become an Angel of Life.

Quite the opposite of Woe.

So what's the message? Can both destinies occur simultaneously? Yes. Both fates are options for us to choose, using our free will.

How do we control our fate? How do we ensure that we find ourselves in the universe of Blessed as opposed to the universe of Woe?

The game is going to end, no matter what. We are going to achieve our ultimate destiny of happiness. Our free will decides *how* we're going to get there. We can remove Bread of Shame through constant suffering. Or we can achieve our purpose by overcoming ego through proactive practice and arrive at fulfillment through our own effort.

The circumstances of our lives and global conditions will depend upon the individual and collective actions of humankind. The state of the world is merely the sum total of the interactions of its inhabitants. Black holes in space, tornadoes in Oklahoma, sunny days, calm seas, peace among nations, available parking spaces—everything rides on the interactions between one human being and another.

The *Zohar* teaches that the Earth is the center of the universe and that our spiritual actions, reactive or proactive, drive the cosmos. From our dearest friends to our worst enemies, we are all connected on a deeper level of reality.

When the accumulated intolerant actions of humans become numerous enough, they create a mass of negativity that blocks the Light of the 99 Percent from flowing into our 1 Percent World. This is how chaos is born. The simple, reactive act of yelling at our friend, speaking abusively to our spouse, or cheating someone in business tilts the entire world to the side of Woe. By the same measure, each act of Resistance tilts *all existence* toward the side of Blessed.

Now we know that violence in the world is not random. Disease is not an aimless occurrence. Terrorism is not mistaken madness. Earthquakes are not acts of God. All negative phenomena are born within the darkness created by our collective reactive behavior. Knowing and incorporating this difficult truth within our being is not easy, but it is the *prerequisite* to effecting real change.

Remember what we learned in the opening chapters of this book: Physical creation came about when we, the collective souls of humanity, *rejected* the endless Light of fulfillment that was originally bestowed upon us by the Creator. We did this to gain the opportunity to earn and create fulfillment through our own effort. Moreover, just as an athlete requires competition to give meaning to the concept of victory, the Opponent was created to challenge us during this process.

The Opponent will use time to delay the rewards of good behavior so that we will believe, mistakenly, that goodness does not pay off. The Opponent will use time to delay the payback caused by reactive behavior so that we'll believe, erroneously, that life lacks true justice.

We can now use the wisdom and insight that we have learned to expose this illusion and see the bigger picture. The path to the final result of eternal world peace is ours to choose: self-indulgent egocentric living or spiritual transformation, Woe or Blessed.

According to the *Zohar*, both realities will exist side by side now in the 21st century. The gray areas of life will vanish. A line will be drawn in the sand. Those who embrace spiritual transformation—moving from reactive behavior to proactive—will dwell in a bubble of serenity, even though the world around them might collapse into rubble and ruin.

This is the promise of Kabbalah.

The choice is ours. It always has been.

and, in the end....

Trying to live our lives with complete accountability is perhaps the most difficult of all tasks. It is so much easier for us to take up causes, to try to change the world, instead of looking inward and trying to change ourselves.

The Opponent will be there every step of the way, putting temptation in our path. It will feel so much better to find wrong in others than to look in the mirror and find those same wrongs in ourselves. It is so much easier to be an activist waging war against all the corruption *out there* than to be an activist who battles to change all those hidden egocentric impulses concealed *in here.*

If there is poverty in the world, it means we still have a measure of greed in our own soul. If there is a murder committed anywhere in the world, it means we still speak unkind words when we lose our temper. If there is abuse and corruption before our eyes, either on TV or in person, it means there is still a part of us that enjoys the negative impulses of our ego, no matter how pure, righteous, and well-intentioned we believe we are.

The Opponent blinds us to our own faults. We find it extremely difficult to detect them, let alone admit to them. So here is some advice from the masters who have gone before us.

No longer can we consider ourselves victims

From this point onward, we must accept responsibility for the bad stuff that happens in our life. We must admit that we are the cause. We must realize that we alone, by way of our previous actions, knowingly or unknowingly, have invited situations and people into our lives that will illuminate and bring out all of our destructive traits that we came here to transform.

This awareness represents a profound and dramatic shift in human consciousness. It goes against every inclination and natural tendency in our nature. It means that we are the creators of every chaotic or blessed moment in our life. It means that we recognize ourselves as the cause of our own misfortune or fortune.

Remember, being the cause is one of the main attributes of being proactive. And as we've learned throughout this book, becoming proactive is the ultimate purpose of our existence.

When we transcend the power of impulse, when we rise above the compelling force of animal instinct, when we stop pointing the finger of blame at someone else and, instead, clench a fist and strike a stunning blow to the real Opponent in the game of life, we will make contact with the 99 Percent Realm.

We will connect ourselves to an infinite, endless emanation of Light, invoking the infinite power of God in our life. And then we will see that the awesome power to change anything and everything has been placed in the palms of our hands.

people are mirrors

Imagine a mirror that reflected all your negative character traits, all the reactive instincts you came to this world to transform. Now suppose you smashed the mirror into 1000 little pieces and each piece reflected a different negative characteristic of your nature. Now suppose you scattered all those pieces all over the place.

Guess what? All the negative people in your life, all the negative situations and obstacles that you confront or witness on the evening news, all the things you see wrong in others, are merely pieces of that mirror. Each fragment represents a different reflection of your own character.

When you fix a particular piece of your character, a fragment of mirror will reflect this transformation. You will begin to see the positive aspects of other people. Situations will begin to change for the better. People will become nicer. More caring. More loving. More genuine. And some negative aspects of the external world will change in very tangible ways.

Remember that everything in your life is there for one reason and one reason only: to offer you the opportunity to transform.

Transformation is the only way to effect positive change both in your life and in this world. Stop wasting your energy finding fault in others. Start the transformation within. Start looking for the uncomfortable situations in life and avoid the easy routes. Light will be found only in the storms and rough waters of life. Why? Because choppy seas trigger reactions.

Sure, it will be turbulent for a while. You'll be buffeted from all sides at first. But if you remain certain that you are only being tested and if you don't react, the seas will calm down quickly. And this is when you'll come to know the power of Kabbalah. This is when you'll experience the extraordinary Light that has been trying to reach you and give you everything you've ever desired since time began.

And so we come to the Twelfth Principle of Kabbalah:

Principle Twelve:
All of the Negative Traits that You Spot in Others Are Merely a Reflection of Your Own Negative Traits. Only By Changing Yourself Can You See a Change in Others.

when all is said and done

If you have trouble remembering all the lessons laid out in this book, you will find it reassuring to know that Kabbalah has given us one unique bit of wisdom that contains all the other principles within it. It's a magic secret that goes something like this:

"Love thy neighbor as thyself.
All the rest is mere commentary.
Now go and learn."

When Jesus was asked, "Master, which is the great commandment in the law?" Jesus said unto him, Thou shalt love the Lord thy God with all thy heart, and with all thy soul, and with all thy mind. This is the first and great commandment. And the second is like unto it, Thou shalt love thy neighbor as thyself. On these two commandments hang all the law and the prophets. (Matthew 22:36-40, King James Version)

The Thirteenth (and last) Principle of Kabbalah in this book has a special gift: It contains all the rest.

> Principle Thirteen:
> **"Love Thy Neighbor as Thyself. All the Rest is Mere Commentary. Now Go and Learn."**

More Books That Can Help You Bring the
Wisdom of Kabbalah into your Life

Satan
By Yehuda Berg

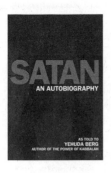

It's said that the greatest trick "the Devil" ever pulled was convincing us that he doesn't exist. In this book, Yehuda Berg uses the device of an "as told to" autobiography to explain the concept of the Adversary which plays a major role in Kabbalistic wisdom. We learn that Satan resides within everyone, manifesting as a recurrent little voice of uncertainty and negativity, and that this is how havoc is wreaked throughout the world. By doing the spiritual work that Kabbalah teaches we can banish doubt and evil influences from our lives and eliminate chaos from the world. Although Yehuda takes creative license with the narrative, he presents a truthful representation of Kabbalah's view on the force of evil in the physical universe.

True Prosperity
By Yehuda Berg

Money is spiritual and its attainment involves utilizing a business plan the universe has blueprinted for us. In *True Prosperity*, Yehuda Berg reveals the secret key to abundance: be the cause and not the effect in life. This entails taking responsibility, breaking chains of routine thinking and guilt, and using stress as a surfboard to ride to new levels of wealth and achievement. By arming oneself with certainty we can overcome the Competitor (code word for Ego), and continually be at the right place at the right time, and making the right business decisions. Yehuda shows how to use goals strategically and flexibly to create abundance in all areas of life. This book is a must-read for spiritually-minded bosses wanting to build a truly prosperous company where every employee finds fulfillment. Utilizing these principles will help to draw down more money from the universe, as well more joy and a world that works better for everyone.

God Wears Lipstick
By Karen Berg

The groundbreaking and bestselling book that revealed the secrets of Kabbalah to women after being forbidden for 4,000 years. For millennia, Kabbalah had not only been skewed towards Jewish men over 40, but everyone including and especially women had literally been forbidden to study it. Kabbalist Karen Berg broke all barriers when she opened the doors of The Kabbalah Centre in 1971 to anyone who had a desire to study. This book was first published to wide acclaim in 2005. Karen unveils the methodology of kabbalistic power that's innate to every woman. She shows how this ancient wisdom explains life's deeper meaning and gives tangible solutions to issues women face today. This book covers how to reach one's highest potential; attract a compatible mate; keep the magic alive long after the honeymoon; create a fulfilling sex life; use astrology to strengthen relationships; know when to leave a relationship, and how to cope when the other partner leaves.

Becoming Like God
By Michael Berg

The ultimate self-help book; it's tough to get better than being like God. New in paperback, from the bestselling author of *The Secret*, comes a revolutionary method for becoming all powerful. Written with extraordinary clarity, Michael Berg presents a logical approach to achieving our supreme birthright. In revealing this opportunity for humanity, he highlights ways to develop our natural God-like attributes and diminish the aspects of our nature that interfere with our destiny. In his succinct style, Michael provides the answer to the eternal question of why we are here: to become like God.

Energy of the Hebrew Letters
By Rav Berg

THE ENERGY OF
HEBREW LETTERS
RAV BERG

Each letter of the Hebrew alphabet transfers awesome power from the Upper World to our physical dimension. Yet only one would be found to contain the attributes necessary to trigger the cosmic event that would propel the unseen world into the realm of material reality. As many know, the Bet was chosen. It is the first letter, of the first word, of the first story in the first book of the Five Books of Moses.

Kabbalists teach that letters of the Hebrew alphabet are, like wires, a technology for transferring energy from the Light of God into the physical world. The story of the letters as they pleaded their respective cases for the primary role in God's creative process is the blueprint by which Creation was made possible. Rav Berg illustrates the bedrock of Kabbalah and poetically reveals the spiritual meaning and history of each of the twenty-two letters: how and why it was created, and what energy it transmits to us.

At a time in which physicists and metaphysicists are joining hands and minds, the Rav uses the story to throw light onto some of the most vexing problems of the present age of quarks, quasars, and quantum mechanics.

The Kabbalah Centre

The Kabbalah Centre is a non-for-profit organization dedicated to bringing the wisdom of Kabbalah to the world. The Centre has existed for more than 80 years, but its teaching lineage extends back to the 16th century and even further back to the *Zohar*, more than 2,000 years ago.

The Kabbalah Centre was founded in 1922 by Rav Yehuda Ashlag, one of the greatest kabbalists of the 20th Century. When Rav Ashlag left this world, leadership of The Kabbalah Centre was handed/given over to his student, Rav Yehuda Brandwein. Before his passing, Rav Brandwein designated Rav Berg as director of The Kabbalah Centre. Now, for more than 40 years, The Kabbalah Centre has been under the direction of Rav Berg, his wife Karen Berg, and their sons, Yehuda Berg and Michael Berg.

The mission of The Kabbalah Centre is to make the practical tools and spiritual teachings available to everyone as a way of creating a better life.

Local Kabbalah Centres around the world offer lectures, classes, study groups, holiday celebrations, services and community activities including neighborhood volunteer projects. To find a Centre near you, visit to www.kabbalah.com.

Kabbalah University

Kabbalah University (www.ukabbalah.com) is an online resource center and community offering a library of wisdom spanning 30 years and rapidly growing. Removing any time-space limitation this virtual Kabbalah Centre presents the same courses and spiritual connections as the physical centers with an added benefit of live streaming videos from worldwide travels.

For a low monthly access fee, as close as a click of your finger, stay current with historic lessons from Rav Berg and inspiring talks with Karen. Delve deeper into Michael Berg's teachings, and journey with Yehuda Berg to holy sites. Connect with world-renowned Kabbalah instructors sharing weekly *Zohar* and consciousness classes that awaken insights into essential life matters such as: relationships, health, prosperity, reincarnation, parenting, and astrology. Check out the hundreds of spiritual topics going back more than four decades. A richer world awaits your presence at ukabbalah.com.

Student Support

On the journey to personal growth it is often helpful to have a coach or teacher. With more than 300 teachers internationally, serving over 100 locations around the world in 20 languages, there is always a teacher for everyone and an answer for every question. All Student Support instructors have studied Kabbalah under the direct supervision of Kabbalist Rav Berg. For more information call 1 800 KABBALAH.

Composed more than 2,000 years ago, the 23-volume *Zohar* is a commentary on biblical and spiritual matters written in the form of conversations among teachers. It was given to all humankind by the Creator to bring us protection, to connect us with the Creator's Light, and ultimately to fulfill our birthright of transformation. The *Zohar* is an effective tool for achieving our purpose in life.

More than eighty years ago, when The Kabbalah Centre was founded, the *Zohar* had virtually disappeared from the world. Today all this has changed. Through the editorial efforts of Michael Berg, the *Zohar* is available in the original Aramaic language and for the first time in English with commentary.

To our parents Solomon and Laura.
When we think of everything they
have done for us, the difficulty becomes
trying to think of something they have not.

Love,
Michael and Tzipa Chaya